John William Mackail

Biblia Innocentium

Being the Story of God's Chosen People before the Coming of our Lord...

John William Mackail

Biblia Innocentium

Being the Story of God's Chosen People before the Coming of our Lord...

ISBN/EAN: 9783337165260

Printed in Europe, USA, Canada, Australia, Japan

Cover: Foto ©Lupo / pixelio.de

More available books at **www.hansebooks.com**

BIBLIA INNOCENTIUM:
BEING THE STORY OF GOD'S CHOSEN PEOPLE BEFORE THE COMING OF OUR LORD JESUS CHRIST UPON EARTH, WRITTEN ANEW FOR CHILDREN BY J. W. MACKAIL, SOMETIME FELLOW OF BALLIOL COLLEGE, OXFORD

NEW IMPRESSION

LONGMANS, GREEN AND CO.
39 PATERNOSTER ROW, LONDON
NEW YORK AND BOMBAY
1899

A LIST OF THE CHAPTERS OF THIS BOOK

I.	The Fall of the Morning Star	*Page* 1
II.	The Six Days of Creation	3
III.	The Garden of Eden	6
IV.	The Serpent in Paradise	8
V.	The Mark of Cain	10
VI.	The Children of Lamech	11
VII.	The World before the Flood	12
VIII.	Noah's Ark	13
IX.	The Bow in the Cloud	15
X.	The World after the Flood	17
XI.	The Tower of Babel	18
XII.	The Shepherd Princes	19
XIII.	The Battle of Four Kings against Five	20
XIV.	The City of Peace	21
XV.	The Promised Land	22
XVI.	The Well in the Wilderness	23
XVII.	The Visit of the Three Angels	24
XVIII.	The Riot in Sodom	27
XIX.	The Pillar of Salt	28
XX.	The Bondwoman and her Son	29
XXI.	The Altar on the Hill-Top	31
XXII.	The Cave in the Field	32
XXIII.	The Camels at the Well	33
XXIV.	The Meeting in the Dusk	35
XXV.	The Mess of Pottage	37
XXVI.	The Dish of Savoury Meat	38
XXVII.	The Anger of Esau	41

	Page
XXVIII. Jacob's Ladder	42
XXIX. The Fair Shepherdess	43
XXX. The Sisters	44
XXXI. Laban's Flocks	45
XXXII. The Flight from Haran	47
XXXIII. The Angel by the River	49
XXXIV. Jacob's Home-Coming	51
XXXV. The Coat of Many Colours	52
XXXVI. The Midianite Merchants	53
XXXVII. Potiphar's Wife	56
XXXVIII. Joseph in Prison	57
XXXIX. King Pharaoh's Dreams	59
XL. The Seven Years of Plenty	61
XLI. The First Journey to Egypt	62
XLII. The Second Journey to Egypt	65
XLIII. The Dinner in Joseph's House	66
XLIV. The Silver Cup	67
XLV. Judah's Pleading	69
XLVI. The Mercy of Joseph	71
XLVII. The Third Journey to Egypt	72
XLVIII. The Grandchildren	73
XLIX. The Mourning in the Meadow	75
L. The Ark of Bulrushes	77
LI. The Exile in the Desert	78
LII. The Burning Bush	80
LIII. The Taskmasters	81
LIV. The Ten Plagues	82
LV. The Passover	85
LVI. The Pillar of Cloud and Fire	86
LVII. The Passage of the Red Sea	87
LVIII. Angels' Bread	89
LIX. The Ten Commandments	91
LX. The Tables of Stone	92
LXI. The Golden Calf	93
LXII. The Tabernacle in the Wilderness	95
LXIII. The Twelve Spies	97
LXIV. The Murmuring in the Wilderness	98

		Page
LXV.	Aaron's Rod	99
LXVI.	The Serpent of Brass	100
LXVII.	The Victories in the Wilderness	101
LXVIII.	Balaam's Ass	102
LXIX.	The Hidden Grave	105
LXX.	The Scarlet Ribbon	106
LXXI.	The Crossing of Jordan	108
LXXII.	The Walls of Jericho	109
LXXIII.	The Ambassadors	111
LXXIV.	The Staying of the Sun and Moon	112
LXXV.	The Days of the Judges	113
LXXVI.	The Iron Chariots	114
LXXVII.	Jael's Hammer	115
LXXVIII.	The Oak in Ophrah	116
LXXIX.	Gideon's Fleece	117
LXXX.	The Choosing of the Three Hundred	118
LXXXI.	The Trumpets at Midnight	119
LXXXII.	The Chase of the Kings	120
LXXXIII.	The Story of the Trees who went out to choose a King	122
LXXXIV.	The Tower of Thisbe	124
LXXXV.	Jephthah's Daughter	125
LXXXVI.	The Lion in the Vineyards	127
LXXXVII.	Samson's Riddle	128
LXXXVIII.	The Gates of Gaza	130
LXXXIX.	The Stolen Secret	131
XC.	Samson's Revenge	133
XCI.	The Famine at Bethlehem	134
XCII.	The Vow of Ruth	135
XCIII.	The Gleaner	136
XCIV.	The Threshing-Floor in the Dark	138
XCV.	The Kinsmen	140
XCVI.	The Child in the Temple	141
XCVII.	The Voice by Night	142
XCVIII.	The Ark in Battle	144
XCIX.	The Terror of the Ark	146
C.	The Lost Asses	148

		Page
CI.	The Street at Dawn	150
CII.	The Gap in the Cliffs	152
CIII.	The Boy Harper	154
CIV.	The Giant's Challenge	155
CV.	The Five Smooth Stones	157
CVI.	The Image under the Counterpane	158
CVII.	The Camp in the Forest	159
CVIII.	The Witch of Endor	161
CIX.	The Woeful Battle on Mount Gilboa	163
CX.	The Stolen Crown	164
CXI.	The Castle of Zion	165
CXII.	The Triumph of the Ark	167
CXIII.	The Thirty Knights	168
CXIV.	The Shot from the Wall	170
CXV.	The Story of the Ewe-Lamb	172
CXVI.	The Sick Child	173
CXVII.	The Rebellion of Absalom	174
CXVIII.	The Flight into the Wilderness	176
CXIX.	The Counsel of Ahithophel	177
CXX.	The Well in the Courtyard	178
CXXI.	The Battle in the Wood	179
CXXII.	The Two Runners	181
CXXIII.	The Sorrowful Victory	182
CXXIV.	The City of Meadows	183
CXXV.	The Watching of Rizpah	184
CXXVI.	The Angel's Sword	186
CXXVII.	The Choice in the Dream	187
CXXVIII.	The Judgment of Solomon	188
CXXIX.	The Glory of Solomon	189
CXXX.	The Building of the Temple	191
CXXXI.	The Feast of the Dedication	192
CXXXII.	The Cedar Palace	193
CXXXIII.	The Queen of Sheba	194
CXXXIV.	The Division of the Kingdoms	195
CXXXV.	The Man of God from Judah	197
CXXXVI.	The Widow's Jar	199
CXXXVII.	The Altars on Mount Carmel	200

CXXXVIII.	The Little Cloud	*Page* 202
CXXXIX.	The Still Small Voice	203
CXL.	Naboth's Vineyard	205
CXLI.	The Council of the Kings	206
CXLII.	The Random Arrow	208
CXLIII.	The Chariot of Fire	209
CXLIV.	The Lady of Shunem	210
CXLV.	The Syrian Captain	212
CXLVI.	The Bags of Silver	213
CXLVII.	The Blind Army	215
CXLVIII.	The Famine in Samaria	216
CXLIX.	The Empty Camp	218
CL.	The Arrows of King Joram	220
CLI.	The Mutiny of the Captains	221
CLII.	The Ride from Ramoth-Gilead	222
CLIII.	The Window over the Gate	223
CLIV.	The Story of the Cedar and the Thistle	225
CLV.	The Assyrian Captivity	226
CLVI.	The Tempest	227
CLVII.	Jonah's Gourd	228
CLVIII.	The Destroying Angel	230
CLIX.	The Graveyard on the Hill	232
CLX.	The Waters of Babylon	233
CLXI.	The Vision of the Cherubim	235
CLXII.	The Vision of the Horses in the Valley	236
CLXIII.	The Vision of the Golden Lamps	237
CLXIV.	The Vision of the Four Chariots	238
CLXV.	The Complaint of the Captives in Babylon	238
CLXVI.	The Valley of Dry Bones	240
CLXVII.	The Magicians	241
CLXVIII.	The Wisdom of Daniel	242
CLXIX.	The Fiery Furnace	244
CLXX.	The Proud King	247
CLXXI.	The Writing on the Wall	248

CLXXII.	The Den of Lions	Page 250
CLXXIII.	The Feast in the Palace of the Lily	252
CLXXIV.	The Malice of Haman	254
CLXXV.	The Golden Sceptre	255
CLXXVI.	The Book of the Chronicles of the Kingdom	257
CLXXVII.	The Banquet in the Queen's Pavilion	259
CLXXVIII.	The Riding of the Posts	260
CLXXIX.	The Return from Babylon	261
CLXXX.	The Ruins at Night	262
CLXXXI.	The Building of the Wall	263
CLXXXII.	The Heathen Host	264
CLXXXIII.	The Valour of Judith	266
CLXXXIV.	The Supper in the Tent	267
CLXXXV.	The Head of Holofernes	269
CLXXXVI.	The Errand of the Archangel	270
CLXXXVII.	The Journey to Media	271
CLXXXVIII.	The Flight of the Evil Spirit	273
CLXXXIX.	The Return from Ecbatana	274
CXC.	The Wages of Raphael	276
CXCI.	The Angel of Accusing	277
CXCII.	The Four Messengers	278
CXCIII.	The Patience of Job	279
CXCIV.	Job's Comforters	280
CXCV.	The Prosperity of Job	282
CXCVI.	The Man in Golden Armour	283
CXCVII.	The King's Elephants	284
CXCVIII.	The Wisdom of the Romans	285
CXCIX.	The Peace of the Empire	286
CC.	The Vision of the Kingdom of the Saints	287

CHAPTER I

THE FALL OF THE MORNING STAR

BEFORE the beginning of the world God was in heaven; about his throne were the angels and archangels and all the heavenly host in their orders, who praised and served God continually. Nearest the throne of God were the seven great archangels, Michael, Gabriel, Raphael, Uriel, Israfiel, and Azrael, and a seventh whose name is now blotted out of the book of life. This last was the brightest of all the heavenly people; he was called Lucifer, the Morning Star, because he was more splendid than all the rest. But he grew proud over his own beauty, and though he was next to God, nothing would content him but to be first of all, and to sit in God's place on the throne. Therefore he plotted to cast down the Most High and become lord in heaven; and a third part of the heavenly host joined him, being dazzled by his brightness and thinking him as great as God. Then there was war in heaven; and the faithful angels, with Michael the archangel as their chief captain, won the victory over Lucifer and the rebel angels, and drove them out of heaven. The crystal walls of heaven opened before them, and the wicked angels poured down out of heaven into the gulf of night. Then Michael and the victorious angels returned into heaven, the walls closed again behind them, and there was peace. But the place nearest the throne of God was empty, and the brightest of the Morning Stars had fallen out of heaven. Then to fill up the dark empty place and restore the splendour of his house, it pleased God to create man. And as Lucifer had fallen from the place next to God through pride, God ordained that man should rise to the place next to God through humility; and that when the time was fulfilled, the Son of God should humble himself and become man, that through him man might be lifted up to heaven and become more glorious than the angels who fell.

CHAPTER II
THE SIX DAYS OF CREATION

IN the beginning God created the heavens and the earth as a dwelling place for man. The earth was without shape or light or substance, void and empty, like a boiling steam of darkness, till the Spirit of God spread out his wings and brooded over it. For six days of creation God wrought on the house of man, to make it perfect. On the first of the six days God said, "Let there be light;" and there was light. He looked at the light and saw that it was good; then he divided it from the darkness, and called the light Day and the darkness Night; between day and night he made Evening to bring peace, and between night and day he made Morning to bring joy; so the evening and the morning were the first day. On the second day God divided the world of waters, parting the waters above from the waters below by the strong arch of the sky which he stretched between. Below the sky there was nothing yet but the steaming waste of waters; above it were the clouds, and the store-houses of the rain and snow; so the evening and the morning were the second day. On the third day God drew the dry land out of the waters below, and gathered them into one place by themselves; and the dry land was Earth, and the waters in the hollows of the land were the Seas. Then he created out of the earth grass and all kinds of plants and trees with their leaves and flowers and fruit; so the evening and the morning were the third day. On the fourth day God created lights in heaven to divide day from night, and to give light on earth, and to be signs of the seasons and the days and the years. He made the two great lamps of light, the sun to be lord of the day, the moon to be lady of the night, and in the night also he set the whole multitude of the stars, which he numbered and named; so the evening and the morning were the fourth day. On the fifth day God created out of the waters all kinds of fishes and birds, and all the creatures that swim or fly; then he blessed the living things which he had made, and commanded them to multiply, so that the waters might be full of fish, and the land full of birds; so the evening and the morning were the fifth day. On the sixth day God created out of the ground all the beasts, both wild and tame, and all the creatures that walk or run or creep upon the land. Thus the house of man was made and furnished: the green earth and the sea, both filled with live things, the sky above them and the waters above the sky, the sun and moon and stars, evening and morning, night and day. Then, seeing that the house was ready and that all was well made and ordered in it, God created man out of the dust of the ground, making him in his own likeness, and breathing his own spirit into him; and he blessed him, and gave him lordship over the whole earth and all that lived in it. Thus God finished the six days of his creation, and on the seventh day he rested from his work and was well pleased, seeing that it was all good; therefore he blessed the seventh day and appointed it to be the day of his rest; and for delight over the new world the Morning Stars sang together, and all the sons of God shouted for joy.

CHAPTER III
THE GARDEN OF EDEN

THE whole earth then was fresh, green, and bright; no rain fell, but a mist rose from the earth daily and watered the ground. But in all the earth the most beautiful place was the Garden of Paradise, which God planted eastward in Eden. A wall ran all round it, with one gate that looked to the rising sun. Inside it a river rose out of the ground, that watered the garden, and then parted into four streams that ran into the four quarters of the world. The first of the four rivers was Pison, which flowed south through Havilah, the land of gold and spice and precious stones; the second was Gihon, which ran west and flowed into the land of the blacks; the third was Hiddekel, which went eastward into Asia; and the fourth was Euphrates. Paradise was planted with every kind of tree that is lovely in leaf, or good for fruit; and in the middle of it two trees grew side by side and rose higher than all the rest, one the tree of the Knowledge of good and evil, the other the tree of Life. In this garden God put the man whom he had created, whose name was Adam, and gave the keeping of it into his charge. All the beasts and birds came in pairs before Adam in the garden, and worshipped him as their master, and he gave them each their own name. But he himself was alone in the garden, and had no companion. Then God made a deep sleep fall on him, and as he slept, took out one of his ribs and closed up the flesh again, and made the rib into a woman; then he brought her to Adam and woke him again out of sleep. Adam at once knew that the woman was sent him to be his wife. He called her Eve, the mother; and Adam and Eve lived in Paradise together, and were without sin or fear or shame. God gave Adam leave to eat the fruit of all the trees in the garden except the apples growing on the tree of the Knowledge of good and evil; he forbade Adam to eat of them, that he might not lose his innocence and die.

CHAPTER IV
THE SERPENT IN PARADISE

OF all the beasts with whom Adam and Eve lived and talked in Paradise, the wisest was the serpent. He asked Eve, "Has God told you not to eat of any tree in the garden?" She answered, "We may eat the fruit of any tree except the tree of the Knowledge of good and evil; but we must not eat that, nor even touch it, or we shall die." He said, "You shall not die: if you eat of it you shall know good and evil, and be as wise as God himself." Eve looked at the tree; it was pleasant to the eye; the fruit seemed good to eat; and in her desire to know good and evil she forgot her obedience. From looking, she fell to wishing; from wishing, to touching; at last she plucked an apple and ate it; then she gave another to Adam, and he ate it also. Till then they had only known good; now they knew good and evil, and the clothing of innocence fell off them. Now they were afraid of God; and trying to conceal their nakedness and shame, they made themselves coverings of fig-leaves, and hid among the trees all the rest of the day. In the cool of the evening God came to walk in the garden, and they heard his voice calling them. They came before him in great fear and misery; and Adam said to God, "I heard the sound of thee in the garden, and was afraid, because I was naked, and hid myself." God said to Adam, "Who told you that you were naked? Have you been eating of the tree of which I told you not to eat?" Adam answered, "The woman whom thou gavest to be with me, she gave me fruit from the tree, and I ate." Then God said to Eve, "What is this that you have done?" She answered, "The serpent beguiled me, and I ate." Then God gave judgment upon all the three. He condemned the serpent to go crawling on the ground and eat dust for ever; and Adam and Eve were sentenced to be driven out of Paradise and not to eat any more of the tree of Life; for it did not grow anywhere except in that garden. Labour and sorrow were sent into their life, and in the end they had to die; the ground was cursed to them, and made to bear thorns and thistles, and only to yield food by hard work and the sweat of Adam's brow; and Eve had to bear her children with sorrow and pain. Then

God clothed them both with coats of skins and drove them out of the garden; and when they left Paradise it was barred behind them, and a guard of angels set at the gate with a flaming sword that turned every way, so that no man thenceforth might be able to go in and eat fruit from the tree of Life.

CHAPTER V
THE MARK OF CAIN

AFTER Adam and Eve were driven out of Paradise they had two children, Cain and Abel; Abel was a shepherd, and Cain a tiller of the ground. But Cain was proud and displeased God; and when they were both making sacrifice to God, Abel of his sheep and lambs, Cain of his fruit and corn, God accepted Abel's offering but refused Cain's. At that Cain's face fell; and when he and his brother Abel were alone in the field, he struck Abel to the ground and killed him, and buried the body, thinking that the murder would never be known. But the voice of Abel's blood cried out of the ground to God; and God called Cain and said to him, "Where is Abel your brother?" Cain lied, and said,

"I do not know; am I my brother's keeper?" Therefore God laid this curse on him, to go on tilling the ground without its yielding anything to him, because he had spilt his brother's blood upon it; and to be a fugitive and vagabond in the earth, and hid from the face of God. Cain said to God, "My punishment is greater than I can bear; I am driven out to wander upon the earth, and any one who finds me will kill me." Then God set a mark upon him, that he might be known, and promised that vengeance should be taken sevenfold upon any one who killed him.

CHAPTER VI
THE CHILDREN OF LAMECH

CAIN went out from the presence of God, and lived alone to the east of Eden, where he built a city and had many children, who peopled that land. Long afterwards one of his family called Lamech, who was old and nearly blind, met something as he went in a wood that he thought was a wild beast, and shot two arrows at it. But this was Cain; and the first arrow shot him dead, and the second killed Lamech's own son. When Lamech found out what he had done, he made great lamentation, crying to his wives, "Hear my voice, O wives of Lamech, listen to my speech; for I have slain a man to my wounding, and a young man to my hurt. If the vengeance for Cain was sevenfold, truly the vengeance for me shall be seventy times seven." Lamech had three sons and a daughter. Two of his sons were called Jabal and Jubal; Jabal was the first of all men to live in tents, and keep herds of cattle; Jubal was the first musician, and invented the harp and pipe. The third son, who was called Tubal-cain, invented the use of metals and was the first workman in brass and iron. But Lamech's daughter Naamah was very beautiful, and became the wife of one of the fallen angels; for many of the fallen angels married daughters of men when they saw them to be fair, and had children, who were the giants and the mighty men of old.

CHAPTER VII
THE WORLD BEFORE THE FLOOD

AFTER Abel was dead and Cain gone away into his banishment, Adam and Eve had many more children, and as time went on the world became full of people. But all the while men grew worse and worse, and turned to wickedness and evil thoughts. Enoch the prophet warned them to beware of God's judgments; but when his warnings were in vain, God took him up alive to heaven in a chariot of fire, and he did not see death. After him lived Noah, who walked with God upon earth. He was a just man, and a good son, and comforted his parents for their work and the toil of their hands. But the wickedness of the rest of the world grew greater and greater continually, and the earth was filled with corruption and violence; so that God determined to destroy them all in the Flood.

CHAPTER VIII
NOAH'S ARK

GOD warned Noah that the Flood was coming to destroy all that was alive on the earth, except Noah himself and his family, and one pair of every kind of creature, which were to be saved along with Noah in an ark. Then at God's bidding Noah began to build the ark of wooden planks and beams, and built at it diligently for years until it was finished. It had three stories, with a door in the side and windows near the top; and was covered with pitch both inside and out, to keep it sound and dry. Noah stored in it food enough to feed himself and his family and all the beasts and birds and creeping things that were to be with them. At last there came a day in spring when the ark was ready; then Noah went into it with his wife and his three sons, Shem, Ham and Japheth, and their three wives, eight persons in all. The creatures followed him in, beasts and birds and creeping things, one pair of each kind; and at the end of a week all were in their places. Then God shut the door of the ark and made it fast. That same day the fountains of the great deep were broken up and the windows of heaven were opened; and for forty days and nights a great rain fell unceasingly, and all the waters under the earth broke their bars and spouted up from below. Soon the ark floated and began to drift on the surface of the water. Before the end of the forty days all the hills were covered with water, and nothing was to be seen but the ark floating on the rainy sea. By midsummer all that had been alive on the earth was drowned, both men and beasts; and the world lay under water for a hundred and fifty days.

CHAPTER IX
THE BOW IN THE CLOUD

THEN the fountains of the deep were stopped and the windows of heaven were shut, and the rain ceased to fall. A clear drying wind rose and blew, and the flood began to ebb, and the water sank lower and lower continually. The peaks of the mountains soon began to show above the flood, and in autumn the ark touched ground on the mountains of Ararat and settled fast there. Still the waters went on sinking. When winter was over, hill-tops could be seen out of the windows of the ark. Then Noah opened the window, and sent out a raven and a dove as messengers to see what news they would bring. The raven flew off and wandered to and fro until the ground was dry, and never came back to Noah; but the dove, finding nowhere to settle, because the face of the earth was still covered with water, came back; and Noah put out his hand at the window and pulled her in again to the ark. After seven days he sent her out again a second time; and in the evening she came back to the ark, carrying in her beak a freshly plucked olive leaf; so Noah knew that the earth was drying up and the trees beginning to grow green again. He waited seven more days and sent the dove out a third time; and this time she flew into the green woods and lived there, and did not come back to him any more. Then Noah set to work and broke open the roof of the ark, and all round him there was dry ground; so he came out of the ark with his wife and children and all the creatures. They had been in the ark a year and ten days. When Noah came out of the ark he built an altar and offered sacrifice to God, who blessed him and his children, and commanded them to increase and fill the earth once again. Also God promised never to send another flood to destroy the earth, and for a token of his promise he made the rainbow and set it in the cloud, that when the clouds brought rain men might see the rainbow in them and take courage, knowing that a new flood was not coming to drown the world.

CHAPTER X
THE WORLD AFTER THE FLOOD

BUT the flood had swept over the garden of Paradise, and thrown down the wall, and left it bare and open like the rest of the earth, and washed away the Tree of Life; so that the guard of angels with the flaming sword were not there any more. In the flood also died Methusaleh, the son of the prophet Enoch, who had the longest life of any man who has ever lived, nine hundred and sixty-nine years. After the flood Noah became a husbandman; also he planted the first vineyards and made wine; and the world grew to be peopled again as it had been before the flood. In those days lived Nimrod, who was a mighty hunter before the Lord. He was the first of the great kings of the world; the beginning of his kingdom was in Babylon; and out of that land he went into Assyria and built himself a city, and called it Nineveh.

CHAPTER XI
THE TOWER OF BABEL

THE whole world then were of one race and spoke one language. As they journeyed all together from the East, they came to the plain of Babel in the land of Shinar and settled in it. There they dug clay and burned it into bricks, and made mortar from bitumen, and in the pride of their hearts they began to build a city with a vast tower, which they planned to build up until its top reached heaven, to be a mark for them from vast distances all across the land, that they might not wander, and be scattered abroad over the face of the earth. But as they were building it, God sent confusion of tongues among them, so that they did not understand one another's speech; and they left off building the city, and were scattered over the face of all the earth. But the half-built tower of Confusion was left standing there in the middle of the plain, until little by little the sun and the rains crumbled it away.

CHAPTER XII
THE SHEPHERD PRINCES

THERE were three brothers called Abraham, Nahor, and Haran, who all lived together and fed their flocks on the eastern hills beyond the river, in Ur of the Chaldees. There Haran died, leaving a son called Lot to inherit his share of the flocks; and afterwards Abraham and Lot went westward to seek a new home, while Nahor stayed in Ur. Between the river and the sea lay the land of Canaan, a pleasant country full of corn and wine and olives and honey, watered by rivers and wells, and set between great mountains on the north and the rocks and sands of the southern desert. Abraham and Lot crossed the river and passed into the land of Canaan, and lived there in tents under a tree or by a well, moving with their flocks and herds from one pasture to another, and so travelling slowly down the country towards the south. A time of famine came, when they went into Egypt and lived there till the famine was over; then they returned with such a quantity of flocks and herds that one pasture could not hold them all; so they separated, and Abraham gave Lot the first choice of land. Lot looked about him, and seeing the plain of Jordan to be well watered and like a garden of God, he chose to live there, and pitched his tents among the five Cities of the Plain, near Sodom; but Abraham remained at Bethel, among the hills of the midland. When Lot was gone, God said to Abraham, " Lift up your eyes and look from this hill northward and southward and eastward and westward; all the land which you see I will give to you and to your children for ever."

CHAPTER XIII
THE BATTLE OF FOUR KINGS AGAINST FIVE

IN the days of Amraphel king of Shinar, Arioch king of Ellasar, Chedorlaomer king of Elam, and Tidal king of nations, these four kings made war with the five kings of the Cities of the Plain, the king of Sodom, the king of Gomorrah, and the kings of Admah, Zeboiim, and Zoar. For twelve years the five cities obeyed Chedorlaomer, but in the thirteenth year they rebelled. In the fourteenth year Chedorlaomer and the kings that were with him came with an army, and conquered the giants in the lowlands and the cave-dwellers in the wilderness, and as they returned through the plain, the kings of the five Cities of the Plain went out to battle against them; and they joined battle in the vale of Siddim, four kings with five. There the five kings were beaten by the four, and fled to the mountains; and the kings of Sodom and Gomorrah fell in the flight among the naphtha-pits. Then the four kings plundered the five cities and went on their way, carrying off Lot among their prisoners.

CHAPTER XIV

THE CITY OF PEACE

WHEN Abraham heard the news of this battle and of Lot being taken prisoner, he armed his household servants and pursued the four kings; and coming on their camp suddenly by night in two bands, surprised and routed them, and rescued Lot and all the prisoners. As Abraham returned, Melchizedek the king of Salem came out of his City of Peace to meet him. He was priest of the most high God, and had neither parents nor children, and neither beginning of days nor end of life, but lived in the City of Peace for ever. He blessed Abraham, and gave him bread and wine. Then the king of Sodom came, and begged Abraham to keep all the plunder and only give him back his people who had been taken prisoners. But Abraham gave him everything back, and would not keep for himself so much as a thread or a shoe-latchet out of all that he had taken; then he went back to his home in the hills, and Lot lived in a house in Sodom.

CHAPTER XV
THE PROMISED LAND

ABRAHAM began to grow old, and had no children; therefore he cried to God, and said, "Lord God, what wilt thou give me? for I shall die childless, and my steward, Eliezer of Damascus, possess my house." But God brought him out of his tent into the clear night, and said, "Look at the sky and number the stars in it, if you are able; so many shall your children be. I am the Lord that brought you out of Ur of the Chaldees, to give you this land to inherit it." Abraham answered, " Lord God, how shall I know that I shall inherit it ? " Then a deep sleep came on him as he waited, and a horror of great darkness fell on him ; and in the darkness God spoke, and said, " Know that your children shall be strangers and servants in a land that is not theirs, and shall be afflicted four hundred years ; then I will judge the nation that holds them in bondage, and they shall come out with great riches ; and in the fourth generation they shall return again to this land, for the time is not full till then." After God had spoken thus, a smoking furnace and a burning lamp passed before Abraham through the darkness, and the voice of God spoke once more and said, " To your children have I given this land."

CHAPTER XVI

THE WELL IN THE WILDERNESS

WHILE Abraham and Sarah his wife still had no child and were waiting for the promise of God to come, there was an Egyptian maid called Hagar in the household, who was going to have a child, and because of this she despised her mistress; and then Sarah treated her so harshly that she ran away into the wilderness. As she sat by a roadside well in the wilderness, an angel of God appeared to her and said to her, "Return and submit yourself to Sarah your mistress; for you shall have a son, who will grow up to be a wild man living in the east, and twelve princes and a great nation shall descend from him." Then Hagar returned out of the wilderness, and soon afterwards she had a son, who was called Ishmael. But that well in the wilderness was called thence, the well of the Sight of the Living One; for Hagar said, "Do I still live after seeing God?"

CHAPTER XVII
THE VISIT OF THE THREE ANGELS

IT was in the heat of the day, and Abraham was sitting in the door of his tent under the great oak on the plain of Mamre, when he looked up and saw three strangers coming on foot across the plain. He rose from the tent-door and ran to meet them, and welcomed them courteously, asking them to stay and rest under the tree and eat a morsel of bread before they went on. So they stopped and sat down in the cool of the tent. Then Sarah baked cakes upon the hearth, and Abraham chose a calf from the herd and had it dressed, and brought butter and milk, and stood by the strangers while they sat and ate under the tree. Now these three strangers were angels, but Abraham did not know it. When the heat of the day was over, they rose up and set their faces toward Sodom; and Abraham went with them to bring them on their way. As they went, one of the three strangers stopped and said to Abraham, "The cry of Sodom and Gomorrah is great, and their sin is very grievous; I am going now to see whether they have done altogether according to the cry which is come to me; if not, I will know." Meanwhile the other two had turned away and gone on towards Sodom. Then Abraham knew that he was a great angel, and drew nearer and said, "Wilt thou also destroy the righteous with the wicked? Perhaps there are fifty righteous men within the city; wilt thou not spare the place for the fifty righteous that are therein?" The sun was going down, and the angel answered, "If I find in Sodom fifty righteous within the city, then I will spare all the place for their sake." Then Abraham said, "I have taken upon me to speak unto my lord, I who am but dust and ashes. Perhaps there may lack five of the fifty righteous; wilt thou destroy all the city for lack of five?" He said, "If I find there forty and five I will not destroy it." The sun sank a little lower, and Abraham spoke again: "Perhaps there shall be only forty found there." The angel answered, "I will not do it for forty's sake." Then he said, "Oh, let not my lord be angry, and I will speak: perhaps there shall be but thirty found in it." The angel answered, "I will not do it if I find thirty there." Then he said once more, "Behold now, I have taken upon me to speak to my lord: perhaps there shall be twenty found there." The angel answered, "I will not destroy it for twenty's sake." Then for the last time Abraham said, "Oh, let not my lord be angry, and I will speak yet but this once: perhaps ten shall be found there." The angel answered, "I will not destroy it for ten's sake;" and as the sun set, he passed out of sight, and Abraham returned home.

CHAPTER XVIII
THE RIOT IN SODOM

AT dusk that same evening the two angels came to Sodom, and there Lot sat in the city gate. He rose up to meet them and bowed to the ground, and prayed them to stay the night in his house. They excused themselves at first, and said, "We will lodge in the street," but he would take no refusal; so they went home with him, and he made them a feast. But late at night, before they lay down to rest, the whole mob of Sodom, old and young, came round the house and shouted to Lot, "Where are the men who came here to night? Bring them out." Lot went out, shutting the door behind him, and tried to pacify the people. But they refused to listen, crying, "Stand back," and "This fellow is a stranger here, and he will needs play the judge," and threatening to make it worse for him than for the strangers; and at last they made a rush at the door to break it open. Then the two angels coming to the door pulled Lot in and shut the door again behind him, and struck all the people outside with blindness, so that they went about till they were weary and could not find the door, but raged vainly in the street all night.

CHAPTER XIX
THE PILLAR OF SALT

THEN the angels said to Lot, "Have you any here besides? If so, bring them out of this place; for the cry of Sodom is grown great before the face of God, and he has sent us to destroy it." Lot had a wife and two daughters at home, and two other daughters who were married and lived in the town; he went to their houses and woke them in the night, that they might fly with him; but they would not believe he was in earnest. So the rest of the night was soon gone; and at break of dawn the angels hastened him, and bade him be gone at once as he was; and while he still lingered they took him and his wife and his two daughters by the hand and dragged them out of the town, and there bade him escape for his life and not look behind him or stand still in all the plain, but hasten to the mountain, lest he should be swept away. Lot said, "Oh, not so, my lord; we cannot reach the mountain before the destruction overtake us, but yonder close by is the city of Zoar, and it is a very little one ; may we escape to it, and live ? " The angel answered, " This also is granted you ; make haste, and escape thither ; for after sunrise we cannot delay any longer, and now it is clear day." So Lot fled across the plain, and the sun rose over the earth as he entered Zoar ; and then a rain of fire fell from heaven upon Sodom and Gomorrah, and overthrew the cities and destroyed the whole land, so that there was not a live soul nor a green, blade left in all the plain. Lot's wife neglected the angel's warning, and lingered outside Zoar to look behind her at Sodom ; and she was caught in the rain of fire, and turned into a pillar of salt. When Abraham rose that morning, and looked from his tent towards the land of the plain, he saw the smoke of the country going up like the smoke of a furnace.

CHAPTER XX
THE BONDWOMAN AND HER SON

A YEAR after the visit of the three angels, Abraham and Sarah had a son born, whom they called Isaac. By this time Ishmael the son of Hagar was a boy of fourteen; and when Sarah saw him playing by the tents, she became jealous, and said to Abraham, "Send away that slave-woman and her son into the wilderness, for he shall not inherit along with a son of mine." Abraham was sorry to do this, but saw no help for it; therefore early in the morning he rose and sent away Hagar and her boy, with some bread and a leather bottle of water which she carried on her shoulder. They wandered in the wilderness till the bottle was empty, and they could find no more water, and began to faint for thirst. At last in despair Hagar laid Ishmael under a bush, and went and sat down about a bow-shot off, that she might not see him die, and wept aloud. But God heard the crying of the boy, and an angel called to Hagar out of heaven, saying, "Do not fear, for your boy shall live, and a great nation come of him, and twelve princes who shall build castles and towns in all the waste country of the south." Then God opened her eyes, and she saw a well of water close by, where she filled her bottle and gave her boy drink; and he lived, and grew up, and became an archer in the wilderness.

CHAPTER XXI
THE ALTAR ON THE HILL-TOP

GOD proved Abraham, and said to him, "Take now your son, your only son Isaac, whom you love, and go to a land that I will show you, and offer him there for a burnt offering upon the mountain top." Early in the morning Abraham rose and saddled his ass, and rode away with Isaac and two servants. They went through the land for three days; and on the third day Abraham saw far off a shining mountain top and knew it for the place that God had told him of. He said to his men, "Stay here, while I and the boy go yonder and worship, and we will come back again to you." So Abraham and Isaac left the two servants with the ass at the bottom of the mountain, and began to climb up on foot, Isaac carrying the bundle of faggots, and Abraham the fire. Then Isaac said, "Father, here are the fire and the wood, but where is the lamb for the burnt offering?" Abraham answered, "My son, God himself will provide the lamb;" and they went on together. When they came to the hill-top

Abraham built an altar there, and laid the wood in order on it; then he bound Isaac and laid him on the altar. But as he took the knife in his hand an angel called to him out of heaven, "Do not lay hand on the boy, to do him harm." Then Abraham looked up, and close behind him he saw a ram caught by his horns in a thicket, which he took and offered up to God; then he and Isaac went down the hill again and rode home.

CHAPTER XXII
THE CAVE IN THE FIELD

SARAH fell ill and died in the city of Hebron, and Abraham mourned over her. Then he stood up from before his dead and said to the sons of Heth, who lived in the city, "I am a stranger among you; give me a burying-place that I may bury my dead out of my sight." The sons of Heth answered him, " Hear us, my lord; you are a prince of God among us; take the choice of our burying-places and bury your dead there." Then Abraham stood up and bowed to the people of the land, and said, "Intreat for me then to Ephron the son of Zohar to sell me his field and cave, called

Machpelah, which he has in Hebron." Ephron stood up in the city gate and answered, " My lord, I give you the field and the cave; they are worth four hundred pieces of silver, but what is that between you and me ? " Then Abraham weighed out the full price to Ephron there in the gate, four hundred pieces of silver in good money, and so in presence of all the people the cave of Machpelah with the field and the row of trees planted round it were made sure to him in possession; and there he buried Sarah with great mourning.

CHAPTER XXIII
THE CAMELS AT THE WELL

WHEN Sarah was dead and Abraham very old, he wished, before he died, to find a wife for his son Isaac among their own kindred. He called his steward, Eliezer of Damascus, and said to him, " Go across the river to Haran, where my brother Nahor lives with his people, and bring a wife for my son from there; for he must not marry among the daughters of the land where we dwell." Eliezer said, " What if the woman will not come ? Shall Isaac go back to

Haran and live there?" Abraham answered, "When God brought me to this land, he promised to give it to my children; therefore Isaac must not go back; but God will send his angel with you, that you may bring a wife for my son to this land." So Eliezer went on his journey with servants and ten camels, carrying rich presents with him. After travelling for many days, he came at evening to a little town where the women were drawing water at a well outside the wall. There he made his camels kneel down by the well, and prayed to God to prosper his errand. As the words were in his mouth, a beautiful girl came out of the town gate with her water-jar upon her shoulder, and went down to the well. When she had filled her jar, and come up, he went to meet her and asked her for a drink of water. "Drink, my lord," she said, and let down her jar on her hand to give him drink; and when he had drunk, she said, "I will draw water for the camels too." So she emptied her jar into the trough and ran down again to the well, and drew water till there was enough for all the camels. While they were drinking, Eliezer opened a package and took out two bracelets and a forehead-jewel of gold, and put the bracelets on her arms and the jewel on her forehead, asking her, "Fair maid, whose daughter are you? and is there room in your father's house for me to lodge?" "Yes," she said; "we have corn and straw for the camels, and room for you to lodge in. I am Rebekah, the daughter of Bethuel the son of Nahor." Then Eliezer bowed down and blessed God, because he had brought him straight to the house of his master's brethren.

CHAPTER XXIV
THE MEETING IN THE DUSK

REBEKAH ran home to tell the household, and shewed them the forehead-jewel and the gold bracelets on her hands. Then her brother Laban hastened out to the well, where Eliezer stood by his camels, and brought him to the house. He ungirthed his camels and shook out straw for them and gave them fodder; then they brought him indoors and set out food before him, but he would not eat till he had told his errand. So he told them how God had blessed Abraham and given him great riches; and how Sarah had borne him a son in his old age, who would inherit all he had; and how Abraham would not take a wife for his son from the people of the land, but had sent to find one among his kindred across the river; and of his own journey, and how he had come to the well and prayed God to shew him the woman whom he had appointed, and how he had met Rebekah. "And now," he said, "give me my answer." They answered, "This is the very hand of God; take Rebekah, and let her be your master's son's wife;" and that night they held the feast of betrothal, and Eliezer gave costly presents of gold and silver and stuffs to them all. The next morning he said he must set off at once to go back to his master. They would fain have had Rebekah stay with them for a little while, ten days at the least; but when it was left to her to decide, she said, "I will go now;" and so they gave her their blessing and let her go, taking her nurse and her maidens with her. They crossed the river and travelled back into the south till one day at evening they came in sight of Abraham's tents. Isaac had gone out by the well of the Sight of the Living One, and walked in the field alone, mourning for his mother, when he saw the line of camels coming in the dusk. Rebekah asked Eliezer of Damascus, "What man is this that walks in the field?" and he looked, and answered, "It is my master's son." Then she alighted from her camel and covered her face with her veil. So she became Isaac's wife, and he loved her, and was comforted for his mother's death.

CHAPTER XXV
THE MESS OF POTTAGE

ISAAC and Rebekah had two sons who were twins, and no more children; and soon after they were born, Abraham died at a great age, an old man and full of years, and they buried him in the cave among the trees at Hebron, beside Sarah his wife. After his death God blessed Isaac with the blessing of Abraham, and he lived peaceably in the land of Canaan, going from one place to another, and digging wells and pasturing his flocks and herds. The elder of the twins, who was called Esau, grew up a rough hairy man, a cunning hunter and a man of the field; but the younger, Jacob, was a smooth-faced man who lived indoors and did his business about the tents. Esau was his father's favourite child, and Jacob his mother's. When they were both grown up, Esau came in from a hard day's hunting faint with hunger, and found Jacob in the tent cooking a mess of pottage. He said, " Give me some of that ; " and Jacob said, " You may have it all if you will sell me your birthright for it." Esau was careless and hungry, and said to himself, " What good is my birthright to me ? " so he sold it to Jacob for the mess of pottage ; then he ate and rose up and went his way, thinking no more about it.

CHAPTER XXVI
THE DISH OF SAVOURY MEAT

WHEN Isaac was very old and weak and nearly blind, and did not know when he might die, he called Esau to his bedside and told him, " Take your bow and arrows and go out after game, and dress me a dish of savoury meat such as I love, that I may eat of it and bless you before I die." So Esau took his bow and arrows and went out into the field after game. But Rebekah had heard what Isaac said to him ; and as soon as Esau was gone she said to Jacob, " Do as I tell you : go to the flock and fetch me two good kids, and I will make of them savoury meat for your father such as he loves, and you shall take it to him and have the blessing." For Isaac was so blind that he could not tell one person from another but by their voice or by touching them. Jacob said, "My brother is hairy and I am smooth; if my father feels me and finds out who I am, I shall get his curse and not his blessing." "The curse be on me, my son," said Rebekah; "only do as I tell you and fetch me the kids." So he brought them, and she made a dish of savoury meat. Then she took clothes of Esau's that she kept in the house, and made Jacob put them on, and covered his hands and neck with the rough skins of the kids. When he was dressed up, he took the dish to his father, with bread and wine, and invited him to sit up and eat. Isaac asked, "Who are you?" and he said, "I am Esau your first-born." Isaac said, "How are you back so soon, my son? come near, that I may feel you, whether you be my very son Esau or not." Then Jacob went up to the bed; and Isaac felt him, and said, "The voice is Jacob's voice, but the hands are the hands of Esau; are you my very son Esau?" Jacob answered, "I am;" then he was satisfied, and sat up and ate, and then gave Jacob his blessing: and this was, that he should possess the dew of heaven and the fatness of earth, and have plenty of corn and wine, and be lord over his brethren. Then Jacob went away; and he was hardly gone, when Esau came in from his hunting with his dish of savoury meat, and brought it in to Isaac, saying, "Rise and eat and bless me." Then Isaac trembled greatly, and cried, "I have given my blessing already, and now I cannot take it back." When Esau heard this, he cried out aloud with a bitter cry, "Bless me, even me also, O my father; have you not kept a blessing for me?" But Isaac answered, "See, I have made him your lord, and given him corn and wine; what shall I do now for you, my son?" Esau cried out again, "Have you but one blessing, O my father? Bless me, even me also." Then Isaac blessed him also, as well as he could; but all that he could give him was a dwelling far from the fatness of earth and the dew of heaven; and to live by the sword, and serve his brother, yet not for ever.

CHAPTER XXVII
THE ANGER OF ESAU

THEN Esau, who once had cared so little about his birthright, hated Jacob for having stolen the blessing of the first-born from him, and thought with himself, "When my father is dead, and that will not be long, I will kill Jacob." Rebekah saw what was in his mind, and determined that Jacob must go away out of danger, till Esau's anger was spent and he had forgotten his wrong. "And then," she thought with herself, "I will send and fetch him back again." Now Esau had married one of the daughters of Heth from among the people of the land, and this was a grief of mind to both Isaac and Rebekah; so she complained to Isaac that she was weary of her life because of the daughters of Heth. "If Jacob too were to marry another of them," she said, "it would break my heart; let us send him to Haran to our kindred across the river, that he may take a wife there among his own people, as I was brought to be your wife long ago." Isaac agreed; and they sent Jacob away quietly, going on foot and alone, to the house of his uncle in Haran. But Rebekah never saw him again, for she died before he came back.

CHAPTER XXVIII
JACOB'S LADDER

JACOB travelled all day, till the sun had set and it grew dark; then, as there was no place of shelter near, he wrapped himself in his cloak and lay down in the field, putting a stone under his head for a pillow, and so fell asleep under the open night. As he slept he dreamed, and in his dream he saw a ladder set up with its foot on earth and its top reaching to heaven, and the angels of God went up and down on it. Above it God himself stood, and in his dream Jacob heard God say, " This land on which you lie shall be given to you and to your children, who shall be as many as the dust of the earth; and I myself will be with you and keep you in all places where you go, and in the end I will bring you back to rest in this land." Then Jacob awoke out of his sleep and said to himself, " Surely the Lord is in this place, and I knew it not ; " and he saw the darkness and the stars, and was afraid, and said, "How dreadful is this place! this is none other but the house of God, and this is the gate of heaven." Early with dawn he rose, and taking the stone that his head had lain on, set it up on end for a pillar of memorial, and made a vow that if God kept him safely and gave him bread and clothing and brought him back at last in peace to his home, that stone should be the place of God's house. So the place of Jacob's dream was afterwards called Bethel, the House of God.

CHAPTER XXIX
THE FAIR SHEPHERDESS

JACOB went on his journey and crossed the river and came at last to the land of the people of the east. There he saw a well in the field covered with a great stone, and three flocks of sheep lying by it; for it was the well out of which they watered the flocks. He went up to the shepherds and gave them greeting, asking whence they were, and if they knew Laban the son of Nahor. They answered, "We are shepherds of Haran, and we know Laban. He is well; and see, there is his daughter Rachel coming with her flock of sheep." Jacob said, "Lo, it is yet high day, and it is not time to fold the cattle; water your sheep, and go and feed them." They answered, "We are only waiting for Rachel and her flock, that when she comes, we may roll the stone from the well's mouth and water all the flocks together, and drive them afield." With that Rachel the fair shepherdess came up, leading her flock; and Jacob kissed her, and lifted up his voice and wept, and told her that he was her cousin, Rebekah's son. Rachel ran home and told her father Laban, who came out and embraced Jacob and brought him in; and when Jacob had told all his story, he lived there and kept Laban's flocks in the land of the east.

CHAPTER XXX
THE SISTERS

AFTER a month's time, Laban said to Jacob, "You shall not serve me for nothing, though you are my kinsman; tell me, what shall your wages be?" Now Laban had two daughters, Leah and Rachel, but Rachel was the younger and fairer of the two, and Jacob loved her;

therefore he said to Laban, "I will serve you seven years for your daughter." So he stayed with Laban and served him seven years; and they seemed to him but a few days, for the love he had to Rachel. When the seven years were finished, a feast was made to all the people of the place, and at night Laban brought in the bride to Jacob, covered with a veil. But the next morning by daylight Jacob found that it was Leah, the elder sister, who had been given him instead of his own fair maid Rachel. He went in anger to Laban, saying, "What is this?" Then Laban said, "In our country the younger sister is never given in marriage before the first-born; but if you will serve me other seven years for Rachel, you may have her as well." Jacob could do no nothing better; so he had both Laban's daughters to wife, and kept his flocks and herds for seven years more.

CHAPTER XXXI

LABAN'S FLOCKS

AT the end of the other seven years Jacob wished to go back to his own country; but Laban begged him to stay, and asked him to name his own wages and he should have them; for the flocks and herds, which had been little before Jacob came, had increased into a multitude since they were in his keeping. Jacob agreed to stay, and for his hire he chose to have all the speckled and spotted cattle and the brown sheep and the striped goats for his own; and so he served Laban six years more. But Jacob was so skilful a herdsman that his own sheep and cattle increased more than Laban's and were better and stronger than the others; and so it remained, however they divided them: so that at the end of six years Laban's sons complained that Jacob had taken away all their wealth, and Laban himself was not so friendly to him as before. Therefore Jacob made a plan to be gone suddenly; and his wives took his side, saying, "Since our father gave us to you, we are become strangers here, and have no inheritance in our father's house."

CHAPTER XXXII
THE FLIGHT FROM HARAN

THE time of sheep-shearing came, and Laban was gone to see after some flocks that fed three days' journey off. Then Jacob, taking his opportunity, gathered all his goods and flocks and cattle, and mounted his wives and children on camels, and crossing the river, set forth in haste towards his own land. But Rachel, unknown to Jacob, had stolen Laban's gods and taken them away with her among the household stuff. The third day after, word came to Laban at his sheep-shearing that Jacob was fled. He gathered his kinsmen and pursued him, and at the end of seven days overtook him among the mountains, and said, "What is this that you have done, stealing away from me unawares, and not telling me, that I might kiss my daughters and send you on your way with music and singing and mirth? This is a foolish thing to do; and but that God warned me last night in a dream not to hurt you, you are helpless in my hand. And if you must needs be gone, why have you stolen my gods?" Jacob answered, "I was afraid you would not let your daughters go with me; but I have stolen nothing of yours; I give you leave to search the camp with your kinsmen." Laban searched the tents, but could find nothing, for Rachel had hidden his gods under the saddle of a camel, and sat on it; then Jacob in his turn was angry, and said to Laban, "What wrong have I done? Why have you pursued me so hotly? Now let our kinsmen judge between us. For twenty years I have served you faithfully, fourteen years for your daughters, and six for your cattle, in drought by day, and frost by night; you changed my wages ten times: and now, had not God rebuked you yesternight, you would have taken everything from me and sent me away empty." Then Laban said, "Let us make peace." So they piled a great mound of stones for a memorial, and swore to each other before God that neither of them would ever pass that mound to harm the other. Thereafter they feasted, and early the next morning Laban rose and kissed his daughters and blessed them, and returned into his own land.

CHAPTER XXXIII
THE ANGEL BY THE RIVER

JACOB went on his way, sending messengers before him to Esau, to ask his pardon; and when he lay at Penuel by the ford of the river, they came back, saying they had given Esau the message, and that for answer he was coming himself to meet Jacob, with four hundred men at his back. This news filled Jacob with terror. He prayed to God, "Keep me now, O Lord, as thou hast kept me till now; for I am not worthy of the least of all the mercies that thou hast shewn me since I crossed this brook twenty years ago with nothing but the staff in my hand." Then he chose the best of his sheep, goats, camels, oxen and asses, and sent them on in separate droves with a space between each. When Esau met the first drove and asked the herdsman whose it was and where it was going, he was to answer, "It is a present to my lord Esau from his servant Jacob." The second herdsman, when Esau met him, was to say the same, and the rest in like manner; for so, he thought, Esau might be pacified before he met him. So these separate droves crossed the river by the ford and went forward each in order, and the rest of the camp followed, and late at night he sent his wives and children across last of all. But he remained alone on the other side of the river; and there an angel wrestled with him all night till the breaking of day. At dawn the angel said, "Let me go, for day breaks;" but Jacob answered, "I will not let you go, except you bless me." Then the angel said to him, "As a prince you have had power with God and with man, and have prevailed; and your name henceforth shall be no more Jacob, but Israel, Prince of God." Then Jacob said, "What is your own name?" The angel answered, "Do not ask me my name, for it is secret," and passed away; and at sunrise Jacob crossed the ford of Penuel, and found that he went lame where the angel had touched him on the hollow of the thigh as they wrestled by night.

CHAPTER XXXIV
JACOB'S HOME-COMING

THEN Jacob looked forward and saw Esau coming with his four hundred men, and went on alone in front of the others to meet him, bowing down to the ground before him seven times as he came near. But Esau ran and embraced Jacob and fell on his neck and kissed him, and they both wept. Then Esau asked, "What is the meaning of all the droves I met on my way?" "To find me grace in the sight of my lord," said Jacob; and Esau answered, "I have enough, my brother; keep them." Then Esau said, "Let us go on together, and I will travel with you;" but Jacob excused himself, saying, "My lord, you see that I have children and flocks with me, and I must not overdrive the flocks or tire the little children; let me follow you softly at my own pace." So Esau, after offering Jacob some of his men for a guard, turned and went back home as he had come; and when he was gone, Jacob followed slowly by little journeys. On his way he came to Bethel, where he had dreamed of the ladder;

and there he built an altar, and God came down to him and blessed him and went up again into heaven. As they journeyed on from Bethel, Rachel died near Bethlehem among the corn-fields, leaving a newly-born baby, the last of Jacob's children, who was called Benjamin; and they buried her there by the wayside, and set a pillar over her grave. So at last Jacob came to his old father Isaac at Hebron; and not long afterwards Isaac died, and his sons Esau and Jacob buried him. Thereafter Esau and Jacob parted, because they had so many cattle that one land had not pasture enough for them both. Esau went south towards the desert and lived in the mountains; but Jacob and his twelve sons stayed at Hebron.

CHAPTER XXXV
THE COAT OF MANY COLOURS

JACOB'S favourite among his children was Joseph, the elder son of his dear dead Rachel; for her younger son Benjamin was still a little child. Jacob made Joseph a coat of many colours, and loved him the best; and because of this his other brothers hated him.

When Joseph was a boy he had a dream, and his dream was this: that he and his brothers were binding sheaves in the cornfield, when his sheaf rose and stood upright, and their sheaves set themselves round about and bowed before his sheaf. Afterwards he dreamed again; and this dream was that the sun and the moon and the eleven stars came and bowed down before him. When he told these dreams to his father and brothers, his father chid him, and said, "What foolish dream is this? Shall I and your mother and your eleven brothers bow down to the earth before you?" but nevertheless kept the dream in his mind. But his brothers hated him more than they did before.

CHAPTER XXXVI
THE MIDIANITE MERCHANTS

JOSEPH'S brothers were away feeding their flocks in Shechem, and Jacob sent him to them to see how they all were, and bring him word again. He went from Hebron to Shechem and did not find them there; but as he was wandering in search of them, he met a man who told him he had heard them say that they were going further off to Dothan, where there was a hill with two fountains. Then Joseph went on there, and found them feeding their flocks on the hill. But when his brothers saw him far off, coming over the fields in his coat of many colours, their anger broke out, and they said to one another, "Here comes the dreamer; let us kill him and throw him into a pit, and say that a wild beast has devoured him; then we shall see what becomes of his dreams." They all agreed to this except Reuben, the eldest of Jacob's sons, who pleaded for his life, but he could not prevail on the others. Then he said, "At least shed no blood; cast him into a pit in the wilderness without food or water, and let him die there." He proposed this plan to save Joseph's life, meaning to come back alone to the pit when the others were gone, and take him out and send him back home. The rest agreed to his plan; and when Joseph came, they seized him and stripped off his coat of many colours, and cast him into an empty pit. Then Reuben went away, and the rest sat down to eat. As they were eating, they saw a troop of camels in the distance; and presently a company of Midianite merchantmen came up, who were on their road to Egypt with their camels laden with spicery. Then some one proposed that instead of leaving Joseph to die in the pit to no profit, they should sell him for a slave to the merchants, and so be rid of him; and they all agreed to this; so they drew him up out of the pit and sold him for twenty pieces of silver, and the merchants took him away. When Reuben came back to the pit and found Joseph gone, he rent his clothes, not knowing what had become of him, and cried, "What shall I do? for the child is gone." But the rest had killed a kid and dipped Joseph's coat in its blood, and took it back to Jacob, saying, "We found this lying in the field; is it your son's coat, or not?" Jacob knew the coat, and believed that some wild beast had devoured his son; and he tore his clothes and put on sackcloth and mourned for him many days, refusing to be comforted as long as he should live.

CHAPTER XXXVII
POTIPHAR'S WIFE

THE Midianite merchants carried Joseph into Egypt with them, and sold him for a slave to Potiphar, captain of the guards to Pharaoh king of Egypt. So he served in Potiphar's household, and God was with him, and he did all his work so well that after a while he was made steward, and put in charge over all the house. Now Joseph was very beautiful, and his mistress, Potiphar's wife, cast her eyes on him and would have had his love. But he refused to be false to his master, and though she spoke to him day by day, he would not listen to her, or be with her. At last he went into the house on a day to do his business, when there were none of the people of the house indoors. She found him there alone, and when all her words and wooing were in vain, she caught hold of him by his garment; and he left it in her hands and escaped away. Then her love turned into hatred; she called her servants, and said to them, " This Hebrew slave has been brought into the house to mock me; he came in now and would have done me violence; but when I cried out aloud, he fled and left his garment in my hand." When her husband came home she told the same story to him; and he believed her, and put Joseph into the king's prison; for he was governor of the prison, and it was close by his house. But God gave Joseph favour in the eyes of the keeper of the prison, who treated him kindly, and put him in charge over the rest of the prisoners.

CHAPTER XXXVIII
JOSEPH IN PRISON

WHILE Joseph was in prison, the chief butler and the chief baker in the palace of Pharaoh fell under suspicion of plotting to poison their lord the king, and were put in ward in the same prison; there they lay for a while, and Joseph had charge of them along with the rest of the prisoners. On one night each of them dreamed a strange dream; and when Joseph came in to them in the morning he found them both sad because of their dream, and not able to interpret it. "Tell me what it was you dreamed," he said; and the chief butler began:

"In my dream," he said, "I thought a vine was before me, and on the vine there were three branches; and it seemed to bud and blossom, and ripe grapes came on it. The king's cup was in my hand; and I plucked the grapes and pressed them into the cup, and gave the cup into the king's hand." Then Joseph said, "The interpretation of your dream is this: The three branches are three days; and within three days you shall be restored to your office and give the cup into the king's hand as before. But remember me, I pray you, when it is well with you, and have me delivered out of prison; for I am here for no wrong that I have done." Then the chief baker, when he heard the chief butler's dream so well interpreted, was the readier to tell his own. "In my dream," he said, "I thought I had three baskets of white bread on my head; and in the uppermost basket were all sorts of pastry for the king's table; and the birds came and ate them out of the basket upon my head." Joseph answered him, "The three baskets are three days; within three days Pharaoh shall take your office from you and hang you on a gallows, and the birds shall eat your flesh there." The third day after this was Pharaoh's birthday, when he made a feast to all his household; and on that day the chief butler and the chief baker were both taken out of prison, and the chief butler was restored to his place, to give the cup into the king's hand as before, and the chief baker was hanged, just as Joseph had foretold. Yet the chief butler did not remember Joseph, but forgot him; and he remained in prison.

CHAPTER XXXIX
KING PHARAOH'S DREAMS

TWO years afterwards, king Pharaoh dreamed a dream; and in his dream he stood by the river, when seven fat and goodly cows came up out of it and fed in the meadow. Then after them came up seven others, lean and ugly, and ate up the first seven; and the king awoke. Then he fell asleep and dreamed again, and in his dream seven ears of corn came up on one stalk, plump and good; and after them sprang up seven thin ears blasted with the east wind; and the seven thin ears devoured the seven full ears; and the king awoke out of his dream. In the morning he was troubled, and sent for all the magicians and wise men of Egypt and told them his dream; but none of them could interpret it to him. Then the chief butler remembered Joseph, and told the king of his dream and the chief baker's dream in prison, and how Joseph had interpreted them both, and it had befallen as he had said. Pharaoh sent for Joseph out of prison; and they brought him out hastily, and he shaved and put on clean clothes and came to the palace. Then the king told him his two dreams, and Joseph interpreted them thus: "O king," he said, "the seven cows, and the seven ears of corn that you saw, both mean seven years (for the two dreams are one); and God shews you by the dreams what is about to befal in Egypt. Seven years of great plenty are coming throughout all the land; and after them shall be seven years of famine, so grievous that the years of plenty shall be forgotten; and the doubling of the dream means that this is very certain, and will shortly come to pass. Let Pharaoh therefore look out a wise man and set him over the whole land of Egypt, with officers under him everywhere, to gather the corn that is left over in the seven good years, and lay it up in store-houses in every city in Egypt; and so the people shall have food through the seven years of famine that are to follow."

CHAPTER XL
THE SEVEN YEARS OF PLENTY

THEN King Pharaoh was pleased, and said to his servants, "Who is wiser than this young man himself, to whom God has shewn all these things?" and with that he took the ring from his own hand and put it on Joseph's hand, and gave orders to clothe him in fine linen and put a gold chain about his neck, and made him ride in the second of the royal chariots, next his own, with men going before him and crying to the people, "Bow the knee;" and he made him governor of all Egypt, to be above all men but the king, and married him to a princess, the daughter of the priest of the temple of the Sun. Joseph was thirty years old when he began to rule over Egypt. Seven years of great plenty followed; and Joseph gathered corn and put it in granaries in every city, till there was such great store that he had to leave off keeping count of it. Then followed seven years of dearth; and in all other lands there was famine, but in Egypt there was plenty of bread. For Joseph opened his granaries and sold the corn to the Egyptians, and to the people who came for corn out of other countries where there was famine. As the years of famine went on, the Egyptians sold all their cattle and lands to the king for food, and became the king's chattels, holding their land of him; and the king became owner of the whole land of Egypt.

CHAPTER XLI
THE FIRST JOURNEY TO EGYPT

THE years of famine were in the land of Canaan also; but in the second year Jacob heard that there was corn in Egypt, and told his sons to go thither and buy bread. So his ten sons went to buy corn in Egypt; but his youngest child Benjamin, Joseph's full brother, stayed at home, lest any harm might befal him on the journey. When the ten brothers came to Egypt, they took their places among the crowd that came every day to buy corn of the governor, and when Joseph came out of his palace they bowed down to the ground before him. Joseph knew his brothers at once, and remembered the dreams he had dreamed so many years before, when he was a boy; but they did not know him; for he was dressed as a great lord, and spoke to them in Egyptian through an interpreter. When he saw they did not know him, he made himself strange and spoke roughly to them. "Whence come you?" he said; and they answered, "From the land of Canaan to buy food, my lord." "You are spies," said he. "Nay, my lord," they said; "your servants are come to buy food; we are all one man's sons; we are true men and no spies." "No," said he again; "you are come to see the nakedness of the land." "My lord," they answered, "we were twelve sons of one man in the land of Canaan, and one brother is dead, and the youngest is at home with our father." But Joseph would not listen to them, and put them all in prison for three days. On the third day he called for them and said, "If you are true men, you may go with the corn you came to buy for your household; but you must leave one brother in prison here, and bring me that other youngest brother of whom you speak; so I shall know if your story is true." At this they were greatly troubled, and began to say to one another, "This distress is come upon us because of our brother Joseph when he cried to us for mercy and we would not hear." "Did I not plead with you in vain for his life?" said Reuben; "and now you see how his blood is being required at our hands." All this while Joseph understood every word they said; but they did not know it, for he spoke to them in Egyptian through an interpreter. But Joseph was so moved that he turned away and wept. Then he turned to them again, and passing over Reuben, who was the eldest, he chose Simeon, who was the next in age, to remain in prison, and let the rest go; and he ordered his steward to fill their sacks with corn, and put back their money into the sacks. So they started on their way home. But at night, when they came to their inn, one of them opened his sack to get out some corn, and found his money lying in the sack's mouth. He shewed it to his brothers, and their heart failed them, for they did not know what to think of it. So they went on their journey, and came to their father, and told him all their story; and when they emptied out their sacks of corn, there was a bundle of money in each sack. But Jacob said bitterly to them, "Joseph is gone, and Simeon is gone, and now you wish to take Benjamin from me too, and bring my grey hairs with sorrow to the grave."

CHAPTER XLII
THE SECOND JOURNEY TO EGYPT

THE famine continued in the land; and when the corn that Joseph's brothers had brought with them from Egypt was all done, Jacob told them to go again and buy some more food. But they said that unless they took Benjamin with them it would be useless to go, for the governor would not so much as see them. "Why did you tell him you had a brother at all?" Jacob said; and they answered, "He asked us closely about our home and kindred, and we told him; how could we know that he would tell us to bring our brother to him?" And Judah went on, and said: "Send the lad with me, and let us go, that we may all live, and not die; I will be surety for him; if we had not lingered, we might have been there and back now." At last Jacob consented. "Take Benjamin and go," he said, "and carry with you a present of the fruits of the land for the governor, balm and honey, spices and nuts and almonds; and take back the money that you found in your sacks, as well as fresh money to buy more corn with; and may God Almighty give you mercy before the man, that he may let both Simeon and Benjamin go." So they went again into Egypt.

CHAPTER XLIII
THE DINNER IN JOSEPH'S HOUSE

WHEN Joseph heard that they were come, he told his steward to bring them in to his house, and have dinner ready at noon. When they were brought indoors, they were afraid that they would be charged with having stolen the money they had found in their sacks, and be sold for slaves. They took the money to the steward, and told him how they had found it in their sacks and could not guess how it had got there; but he only said that they had paid him for the corn and need not be afraid. Then he brought Simeon out of prison to them, and they all went into Joseph's house and washed, and got ready their present for the governor; for the steward had told them they were to dine with him. When Joseph came in at noon, they brought him their present and bowed down before him; and he asked them after their father, and said, "Is this your youngest brother of whom you told me?" But as he looked at Benjamin, he could not refrain himself any longer, and went away hastily into his own room and wept. Then he washed his face and came out again; and dinner was served for Joseph at a high table by himself, and for the Egyptians of his household at another, and for the brothers at a third; and what made them wonder most was that they were made to sit exactly in the order of their age. Joseph sent dishes to them from his table, but Benjamin's dish was five times as much as any of the rest; and they ate and drank and were merry.

CHAPTER XLIV
THE SILVER CUP

AFTER dinner, Joseph said to his steward, "Fill their sacks with corn, as much as they can carry, and put my silver cup in the mouth of the sack of the youngest, and send them away as soon as it is light to-morrow morning." So they started at day-break; but before they were far out of the city the steward came riding after them and charged them with having stolen his master's cup. They said, "We know nothing of it; if the cup is found among us, we will all become the governor's slaves, and the one on whom it is found shall be put to death." "No," he said; "not the innocent for the guilty; he on whom the cup is found shall be my slave, and the rest of you go free." Then they unloaded all their sacks and opened them, and he searched them through, beginning with the eldest, and going down to the youngest; and the cup was found in Benjamin's sack. The steward seized Benjamin; and the rest loaded their asses again and returned with him in grief to the city. They found Joseph in his house, and fell on the ground before him. "What deed is this that you have done?" he said. Judah answered, "What shall we say unto my lord? how can we clear ourselves? God has found out our iniquity, and we are all my lord's slaves." "God forbid," Joseph answered; "the man on whom the cup was found shall be my slave; but for you, get you gone in peace to your father." Then Judah came near and spoke to Joseph thus.

CHAPTER XLV
JUDAH'S PLEADING

"O MY lord," said Judah, "let thy servant, I pray thee, speak a word in my lord's ears, and let not thine anger burn against thy servant; for thou art even as Pharaoh. My lord asked his servants, saying: Have you a father, or a brother? and we said unto my lord, We have a father, an old man, and a child of his old age, a little one; and his brother is dead, and he alone is left of his mother, and his father loves him. Then thou saidst unto thy servants: Bring him to me, that I may set mine eyes upon him; and we said unto my lord: The lad cannot leave his father; for if he should leave his father, his father would die. And thou saidst unto thy servants, Except your youngest brother come with you, you shall see my face no more; and when we went back to thy servant our father, we told him the words of my lord. Then our father said: Go again, and buy us a little food; and we said: We cannot go; if our youngest brother be with us, then we will go; for we may not see the man's face except our youngest brother be with us. And thy servant my father said to us: You know that my wife bore me two sons, and the one went out from me, and I said, Surely he is torn in pieces; and I saw him not since; and if you take this other also from me and mischief befal him, you will bring down my grey hairs with sorrow to the grave. Now, therefore, when I come to thy servant my father, and the lad be not with us, he will die, and thy servants shall bring down the grey hairs of thy servant our father with sorrow to the grave: for thy servant became surety for the lad unto my father, saying, If I bring him not unto thee, then I shall bear the blame to my father for ever. Now, therefore, I pray thee, let thy servant abide instead of the lad a bondman to my lord, and let the lad go up with his brethren; for how shall I go to my father, and the lad be not with me? lest I see the evil that shall come on my father."

CHAPTER XLVI
THE MERCY OF JOSEPH

JOSEPH could bear no more; he called out hastily for every one to leave the room, and as soon as he was left alone with his brothers he wept aloud, so that the Egyptians outside heard it, and said to his brothers in their own language, "I am Joseph." They were so frightened that they could not speak; he told them to come near him, and said again, "I am Joseph your brother, whom you sold into Egypt. Do not be grieved nor angry with yourselves that you sold me hither; for God sent me here before you, that I might save your lives; and he has made me lord of Pharaoh's house and ruler throughout all Egypt. Hasten back now to our father and bid him come here with all his household, and I will keep him; for there are still five more years of famine to come. Tell him of all my glory in Egypt, and bring him hither to me." The news quickly came to Pharaoh's palace; the king was pleased, and said, "Let Joseph's father come at once, and he shall have the best of the land of Egypt." Then the brothers went joyfully home, taking with them waggons from Egypt to carry their household stuff, and twenty asses laden with bread and meat and good things for their father by the way. When they came back to Jacob and told him that Joseph was alive and was governor of Egypt, his heart fainted, for he could not believe it; but when he saw the waggons that Joseph had sent, and heard all that he had said, he revived, and said, "It is enough; Joseph my son is yet alive; I will go and see him before I die."

CHAPTER XLVII
THE THIRD JOURNEY TO EGYPT

THEN Jacob took his journey with his whole household, between sixty and seventy persons in all; and when he had come to the border of Canaan, God spoke to him in a vision by night, saying, "Do not fear to go into Egypt; for there I will make your children a great nation, and bring them again thence." So he travelled on across the desert to Egypt, and Judah went on before to tell Joseph, who drove out in his chariot to meet his father, and fell on his neck and wept a good while; and Jacob said, "Now let me die, since I have seen your face." Then Joseph went to the king and told him that his father and all his household were come; and he presented them to the king, who received them kindly and told Joseph to choose the best of the land for them to dwell in, and appoint some of them (for they were all shepherds) to be keepers of the royal flocks. Joseph made them live in the land of Goshen, between the river and the desert, where there was good pasture, and gave them bread through the rest of the years of famine; and they prospered and increased.

CHAPTER XLVIII
THE GRANDCHILDREN

WHEN Jacob felt the time of his death draw near, he called Joseph to him and said, "Promise me, as you are kind and true, not to bury me in Egypt, but to take me home and bury me with my fathers;" and Joseph promised. Not long after, a message came to Joseph that his father was sick, and he went to see him, taking his two boys, Manasseh and Ephraim, with him. Then Jacob gathered his strength and sat up in bed, and said to Joseph, "When

God Almighty appeared to me at Bethel and blessed me, he promised the land of Canaan to me and to my children for ever. Now your two sons shall each have a full share in it as if they were my own children." Then his mind wandered back to old days, "And as for me," he said, "when I was coming home, Rachel died by me in the land of Canaan on the way, when there was yet but a little way to come to Bethlehem; and I buried her there by the road of Bethlehem;" and he looked at Joseph's sons and said, "Who are these?" Joseph said to him, "These are my sons, whom God has given me in this place." Then Jacob said, "Bring them to me, and I will bless them." Joseph took them both and brought them close, holding Manasseh, the first-born, in his left hand towards Jacob's right hand, and Ephraim, the younger, in his right hand towards Jacob's left hand. But Jacob crossed his hands, and laid his right hand on Ephraim's head, and his left on Manasseh's. Then Joseph, thinking he mistook the two boys, would have taken his father's right hand, to remove it to Manasseh's head from Ephraim's, saying, "Not so, my father, this is the first-born." But Jacob said,

" I know, my son, I know; he also shall become a people, and be great; but his younger brother shall be greater than he." Then he blessed them both, and said to Joseph, " Behold, I die; but God shall be with you and bring you back again to the land of your fathers; and in that land I have given you a double portion above your brothers." Thereafter he called all his sons together, and told them what should befal them in the days to come, and blessed them, and charged them to bury him, when he died, in the cave in the field at Hebron, where Abraham and Sarah and Isaac and Rebekah were buried, and where he himself had buried his wife Leah; and when he had made an end of what he had to say, he died, and was gathered to his people.

CHAPTER XLIX
THE MOURNING IN THE MEADOW

JOSEPH wept for his father and kissed him, and closed his eyes; and he commanded that the body should be embalmed; and they mourned for him in Egypt for seventy days. When the days of the mourning were over, Joseph asked leave from the king to go and bury his father at

Hebron as he had promised; and Pharaoh gave him leave. So Joseph and his brothers bore him away, and the court of Pharaoh and the princes of Egypt went with them on horseback and in chariots, as far as the threshing-floor in the meadow of the Egyptians, and there held a great lamentation for seven days; then the Egyptians went back, and Jacob's sons carried his body to Hebron, and buried it in the cave in the field, and returned to Egypt. After Jacob was dead, Joseph's brothers were afraid that he might have only spared them for their father's sake, and might punish them now for their cruelty to him; so they came and fell down before him and prayed him to forgive them. But Joseph wept for pity, and told them to have no fear. "You did indeed devise evil against me," he said, "but God meant it for good, to save many people alive." So Joseph lived in Egypt in great honour; and when he was old and about to die, he told the children of Israel that when the appointed time came, God would visit them and lead them back out of Egypt to their own land; and he took an oath of them to carry his bones with them when they went. So he died, and they embalmed him, and put him in a coffin in Egypt; and his brothers died, and all that generation.

CHAPTER L
THE ARK OF BULRUSHES

THE children of Israel lived for a long time in Egypt, till the land was filled with them; and new kings reigned, and Joseph was forgotten. At last a king arose who oppressed the children of Israel, and set taskmasters over them to make them work in the brick-fields and build cities for him, and made their lives bitter with hard bondage. But the more they were oppressed, the more they grew; therefore the king gave orders that all their male children should be thrown into the river as soon as they were born. Now a man and his wife among the children of Israel had a boy born to them; and the mother kept her baby hidden for three months to save him from the river; but when she could hide him no longer, she made an ark of bulrushes, and putting him in, laid him among the reeds by the river brink; and his sister was set to watch a little way off. As the baby lay there among the reeds, the king's daughter came down from the palace with her maidens to bathe in the river, and saw the ark lying among the reeds as she walked along the river bank; she sent a maid to fetch it; and when it was fetched and opened the baby was crying inside, and she had pity on him. Then his sister came up and asked her, "Princess, shall I go and find a woman to nurse the baby for you?" "Go," said the princess; and she went and fetched her mother, to whom the princess gave her own baby, and said, "Nurse this child for me." The child lived and throve, and when he was grown his mother brought him back to the princess. She adopted him as her son, and called him Moses, that is to say, Drawn out of the river; and he was taught all the wisdom of the Egyptians.

CHAPTER LI

THE EXILE IN THE DESERT

MOSES went out from the palace to look at the labours of his countrymen, and saw one of them being cruelly beaten by an Egyptian. He looked this way and that, and seeing no one else near, he killed the Egyptian and hid him in the sand. The next day, he found two of the children of Israel quarrelling with one another, and rebuked the one who was in the wrong; but the man turned on him and answered, "Who made you a prince and a judge over us? Do you intend to kill me as you killed the Egyptian yesterday?" When Moses found that what he had done was known, he was afraid that Pharaoh might hear of it and put him to death; so he fled away from Egypt and escaped into the Arabian desert, where he sat down by a well. As he sat there, the seven daughters of Jethro, the prince of Midian, brought their flocks to the well; and when they had filled the watering-troughs, shepherds came and would have driven them away; but Moses took their part, and helped them to water their flocks. When they came home their father asked them: "How is it that you are back so soon to-day?" They said, "An Egyptian stranger helped us, and drew water for us." Then he said, "And where is he? why did you leave the man by the well? go back, and ask him to come and eat bread with us." So they brought Moses to the tents; and he stayed there, and afterwards married one of Jethro's daughters, and kept a flock in the desert.

CHAPTER LII
THE BURNING BUSH

MOSES led his flock round behind the desert for pasture, and came with it to Mount Horeb: and there he saw a burning bush on the mountain, all in a flame of fire and yet not consumed. He turned aside to go near and see, when a voice came to him out of the bush and said, "Put off your shoes from off your feet, for the place where you stand is holy ground." So he put off his shoes, and stood barefoot; then God spoke to him out of the burning bush, saying, "I have seen the affliction of my people in Egypt and heard their cry and known their sorrow; and I am come down to deliver them. I am sure that the king of Egypt will not let them go, no, not by a mighty hand; but I will stretch out my arm, and smite Egypt with all my wonders which I will do in the midst of it; go therefore, and lead them out." Moses asked God, "Give me a sign, that the people may believe my message." God said to him, "What is that in your hand?" and he answered, "A rod." Then God told him to throw the rod in his hand upon the ground. When he did so, it became a serpent, and he started back from it, but when he put out his hand and caught it by the tail, it became a rod in his hand again as it was at first. Then Moses returned, and took his wife and children, and the wonderful rod in his hand, and travelled back to Egypt. On the way he met his brother Aaron, who had come to search for him in the desert; and he kissed him, and told him the words and signs of God; then they went together among the children of Israel, who were making bricks in Egypt to build cities for King Pharaoh, and told them how their deliverance was at hand.

CHAPTER LIII
THE TASKMASTERS

AFTER this, Moses and Aaron went to King Pharaoh, and said, "The Lord God of Israel bids you let his people go that they may hold a feast to him in the wilderness." But Pharaoh answered, "Who is the Lord God, that I should obey him? I know him not, nor will I let Israel go. Get you to your tasks, and do not hinder the people from working." The same day, he commanded his taskmasters not to supply any more straw to the children of Israel for making bricks. "Let them go and gather it themselves," he said; "they are idle, therefore they cry, Let us go and hold a feast to our God; let more work be laid on them, and they will not listen to vain talk." So the children of Israel were worse treated than before, for they had to go on making the full number of bricks for their daily task and to gather straw as well, and were beaten if they fell short; and they murmured against Moses and Aaron for having led them into this trouble. Moses cried to God, "Lord, why hast thou sent me? thou hast not delivered thy people at all;" and God answered him, "Now you shall see what I will do; I am the Lord."

CHAPTER LIV

THE TEN PLAGUES

THEN God began to work great signs and wonders in Egypt by the hand of Moses and Aaron, and sent his plagues, one after another, upon Pharaoh and his people, to make them let the children of Israel go. For when

Moses and Aaron had gone again to the king, and he had refused to listen to them, they stood on the brink of the river with the rod that turned into a serpent in their hand, and stretched it out over the river; and the water in the river and in all the ponds and pools was turned into blood, and the fish died and the water could not be drunk; this was the first plague of Egypt. Then they stretched out the rod over the waters a second time; and frogs came up out of the water and covered all the land, so that the houses and beds and ovens and dishes were filled with them. But Pharaoh called his magicians, and they too turned water into blood and made frogs with their enchantments; and he hardened his heart against the two plagues of the water, and would not let the people go. Then Moses and Aaron stretched out the rod over the dust of the land, and a third plague came; for the dust became lice that covered both men and beasts. Pharaoh's magicians tried to do this, but could not; then they told him that it was the work of God. But he was stubborn and would not hear; therefore a fourth plague was sent, swarms of flies that came into the land and filled the houses; and then a fifth, which was a sore sickness upon all the Egyptian sheep and cattle and horses: yet Pharaoh's pride was not broken, and he would not let the people go for the three plagues of the earth. So a sixth plague was sent on him; for Moses and Aaron took handfuls of ashes of the furnace and sprinkled them towards heaven; and it became a small dust in all the air over Egypt, that made boils break out over man and beast. Then a seventh plague followed; Moses stretched forth his rod towards heaven, and there came thunder and lightning and hail, such as never was known before or since in Egypt, and it destroyed the flax and the barley, and beat down all the crops in the fields and broke the trees. Again for the eighth time Moses stretched forth his rod, and all that day and all night an east wind blew, and with the next morning it brought up a cloud of locusts from across the sea, that covered the land and devoured all that the hail had left, so that there was not one green thing left in Egypt: yet Pharaoh kept his pride. Then once more, for the ninth time, Moses stretched forth his hand, and there was a thick darkness, darkness that might be felt, over all Egypt for three days, so that no man saw another, or dared to stir from his place. But Pharaoh's heart was still hardened, and he would not let the people go because of the four plagues of the air. These nine plagues had fallen on all Egypt, except where the children of Israel were; so that all the while the children of Israel had water and pasture and fair weather, and were not vexed by frogs, or lice, or flies, and had no sickness on either man or beast. When a plague came, Pharaoh would send for Moses and promise to let the people go if it were taken away; but when it left off, he hardened his heart again; and after the ninth plague of the three days' darkness, he told Moses to be gone, and not to come in his sight any more, or he would put him to death; and Moses answered him: "You say well; you shall not see my face again."

CHAPTER LV
THE PASSOVER

THEN God said to Moses, "Bid the people make ready to go; for I myself will come down to-night and bring yet one more plague upon the Egyptians, and that shall be the end."

Moses called all the elders of Israel together and said, "Make ready; gather your households to-night, and in each household kill a lamb and roast it, and sup off the roast meat with unleavened bread and bitter herbs, each one of you girt and shod and with staff in hand, as men who are in haste to be gone; for at midnight God will pass through Egypt and smite the Egyptians. When you kill the lamb take a sprig of hyssop and dip it in the blood, and shake it over the lintel and posts of the doorway; and let no one go out at the door till morning; for when the Destroyer goes through the land to-night he will only pass over the houses that have blood on the doors."

CHAPTER LVI
THE PILLAR OF CLOUD AND FIRE

THE children of Israel did as Moses commanded; and at midnight the Destruction of God went out and slew all the first-born in Egypt, from the first-born of Pharaoh that sat on his throne to the first-born of the slave behind the mill; and there was a great cry in Egypt; for in every house there was one dead.

Pharaoh sent hastily for Moses and Aaron in the dark of night and besought them to be gone; and all the Egyptians, thinking themselves as good as dead, were eager for them to go, and brought them gold and silver and raiment to hasten them. So that night before day broke the whole multitude of the children of Israel were on their journey, with their women and children and flocks and herds; and that day and the next they marched on as far as the edge of the wilderness. They carried the bones of Joseph with them in a coffin, as he had bidden when he was dying, a hundred and fifty years before; and the angel of God went before them to lead them on their journey, in a pillar of cloud by day to shew them the way and a pillar of fire by night to give them light.

CHAPTER LVII

THE PASSAGE OF THE RED SEA

FROM the edge of the wilderness the pillar of cloud and fire no longer led them straight forward out of Egypt, but wheeled to the right and led them down between the mountains and the Red Sea, till they came to where the cliffs ran out into the sea and left no passage, and there they encamped on the sea-shore. But when Pharaoh heard of the way they had gone, he thought that they were shut in there, like beasts in a trap, and that if he pursued them he might fall on them and cut them in pieces or drive them back to be slaves in Egypt; so he armed six hundred chariots and a great host of horsemen, and pursued them. When the Egyptian army came in sight, the children of Israel were afraid, and cried out that it was better to be slaves in Egypt than to die in the wilderness. But Moses said, " Do not be afraid; for after to-day you shall never see the Egyptians again; stand still, and see the salvation of the Lord." As night fell, the pillar of cloud and fire removed from before their camp, and went behind it, between them and the camp of the Egyptians, so that it gave light to the children of Israel, but was a cloud and darkness over the Egyptian army and kept them from coming near. Then Moses stretched out his rod over the sea, and the waters were divided, and stood in heaps on each side of a long lane of land; and the children of Israel marched into the midst of the sea upon dry ground with a wall of waters on their right hand and a wall of waters on their left. The Egyptian army passed in after them under the cloud, going slowly because they could not see their way; and before dawn the children of Israel had crossed over and were on land on the other side, and the Egyptians were in the middle of the sea-path, still wrapped in thick darkness, and with the wall of waters to right and left. Then God looked on the Egyptians through the pillar of fire and cloud, and troubled their host, and took off the wheels of their chariots; and they turned confusedly and began to go backward. But as morning broke, Moses stretched out his rod over the sea again, and it returned to its place, covering chariots and horsemen; and Pharaoh and all his army were drowned in the Red Sea.

CHAPTER LVIII
ANGELS' BREAD

THE children of Israel sang a song of victory on the edge of the Red Sea, while the women danced and played on tambourines. Then they set out on their march through the wilderness. But after a few days they began to be hungry and thirsty; for the food they had brought with them out of Egypt was soon done, and they had nothing to drink but the bitter springs and wells of the desert: so that they began to murmur against Moses and to wish themselves back in Egypt, where they had sat by the cooking-pots and eaten their fill of bread. Then God sent manna from heaven to feed them. Early in the morning the glory of God shone in the pillar of cloud, and when the dew that lay on the ground was drunk up by the rising sun, they saw the face of the ground covered with small round grains like coriander-seed, coloured like spice, and tasting like cakes made with flour and honey. They gathered as much of this as they could eat that day, and when the sun grew hot, the rest melted away where it lay on the ground. Every night the manna fell like rain all round their camp, and every morning they gathered their daily food, and ground it in mills or pounded it in a mortar and made cakes of it and it did not keep till the next day. They called it angels' bread, and they fed on it for all the while they were in the wilderness. Also when they had no water, Moses took the wonderful rod which he had stretched out over the river of Egypt and over the Red Sea, and struck a rock in the desert, and water gushed out of the rock enough for all to drink; and this rock followed them and gave them water in all their wanderings. So they journeyed on through the wilderness, eating angels' food day by day, and drinking of the water from the rock that followed them.

CHAPTER LIX
THE TEN COMMANDMENTS

SO they went on their journey, and three months after they had left Egypt they came to Mount Sinai, where God had spoken to Moses out of the burning bush, and encamped on the plain below it for three days. On the morning of the third day a thick cloud came down and rested on the mountain-top, and there were thunders and lightnings and a long loud trumpet-blast out of the cloud; and the whole mountain smoked and shook, and God descended on it in a flame of fire. Then out of the middle of the cloud and thick darkness, among thunderings and lightnings, the voice of God spoke thus, and said: "I AM THE LORD THY GOD WHO HAVE BROUGHT THEE OUT OF THE

LAND OF EGYPT, OUT OF THE HOUSE OF BONDAGE. THOU SHALT HAVE NO OTHER GODS BEFORE ME. THOU SHALT NOT MAKE ANY GRAVEN IMAGE TO BOW DOWN TO NOR SERVE. THOU SHALT NOT TAKE THE NAME OF THE LORD THY GOD FALSELY. REMEMBER THE SABBATH DAY TO KEEP IT HOLY. HONOUR THY FATHER AND THY MOTHER, THAT THY DAYS MAY BE LONG UPON THE LAND. THOU SHALT NOT KILL. THOU SHALT NOT COMMIT ADULTERY. THOU SHALT NOT STEAL. THOU SHALT NOT BEAR FALSE WITNESS. THOU SHALT NOT COVET THY NEIGHBOUR'S HOUSE, NOR HIS WIFE, NOR HIS SERVANT, NOR HIS OX, NOR HIS ASS, NOR ANYTHING THAT IS HIS." The voice of God spoke these words, and ceased.

CHAPTER LX
THE TABLES OF STONE

ALL the people saw the lightnings and felt the earth tremble, and heard the thunder and the noise of the trumpet, and the voice of God giving his ten commandments; and they were afraid, and stood far off. But Moses and Aaron, with seventy of the elders of Israel, went up on to the mountain, and when they had passed through the storm and darkness they saw above them a pavement of sapphire-stone, like the body of heaven in colour and clearness, spread under the feet of God. Then Aaron and the seventy elders went down again to the people; but Moses went higher up to the mountain-top, and the cloud covered him from the sight of the people for forty days and forty nights. While he was there, God gave him laws for the people; and when he came down he brought with him two tables of stone engraved with the writing of God.

CHAPTER LXI
THE GOLDEN CALF

BUT while Moses was on the mountain the people grew weary of waiting for him; till at last they came all together to Aaron, and said, "Make us a god to lead us; for Moses is gone, and no man knows what is become of him." Aaron told the people to take off their gold rings, and lay them in a heap on the ground; then he melted them down in a furnace and cast out of them the figure of a golden calf, which the people set up in the middle of the camp, and began to sing and dance round it, crying, " This is the God of Israel, who brought us out of the land of Egypt." That very day Moses came down from the mountain carrying the two stone tables of God. When he came near the camp, and saw them dancing round the golden calf, he was so angry that he threw the tables down and broke them; then he came swiftly into the camp and took the calf and ground it to powder, and then sprinkled the powder into water and made the people drink it. Then God called him up into the mountain again, and there he wrote the commandments of God on two new tables of stone like the first. When he came down from the mountain where he had spoken with God, his face shone so that no one could look at him.

CHAPTER LXII
THE TABERNACLE IN THE WILDERNESS

WHILE they stayed in Sinai, the children of Israel made a tabernacle to be God's house in their camp, from a pattern that God had shewn Moses on the mountain. It was built of wooden boards plated with gold, and was hung with curtains of blue and purple and scarlet; and the furniture in it was all covered with gold plating, and the lamps and dishes in it of pure gold. In this tabernacle the mercy-seat of God was set between two golden cherubim that spread out their wings over it from each side till wing touched wing above. The voice of God speaking came from off the mercy-seat from between the two cherubim; and under the mercy-seat was an ark, in which were laid the two stone tables written with the words of God. The ark was made of acacia-wood covered inside and out with golden plates and with a rim of gold round the top; and the mercy-seat and cherubim that stood on it were of pure gold. Round the tabernacle was a square courtyard fenced off with linen curtains hung on silver rods.

The whole tabernacle took to pieces, so that they could carry it with them on waggons as they made their journeys; and when they set it up and laid the ark in it, the pillar of cloud and fire settled down on it, and the glory of God filled it. Aaron was appointed high priest of the tabernacle, and they made for him the holy oil of anointing, which was steeped in spices, myrrh and cinnamon and calamus and cassia, and the holy robe of blue and purple and scarlet inwoven with gold thread and clasped at the shoulders with onyx-stones. Over his robe he wore a breastplate set with twelve precious stones engraved with the names of the twelve tribes of Israel, and fastened on his breast with twisted chains of pure gold; and the skirt of his robe was hung with pomegranates and golden bells alternated, a bell and a pomegranate and a bell and a pomegranate all round about. As long as the pillar of cloud and fire rested over the tabernacle, the children of Israel remained in the camp where they were; but when it rose and moved on, then two trumpeters blew an alarm upon silver trumpets, and they broke up their camp, and followed the cloud and the fire through the wilderness. Day by day as the ark set forward, the people sang

"Rise up, Lord, and let thine enemies be scattered, and let them that hate thee flee before thee;" and night by night as it rested, they sang, "Return, O Lord, unto the many thousands of Israel."

CHAPTER LXIII
THE TWELVE SPIES

ALL this while the children of Israel were encamped below mount Sinai; but in the second month of the second year after they came out of Egypt they broke up their camp in Sinai and took their journey through the wilderness till they came to Kadesh, on the southern border of the promised land. There Moses chose twelve men, one from each tribe, and sent them to spy out the land and bring back word whether it were good or bad, and what kind of people lived in it. They went and searched the land, along and across, for forty days, and then came back, bringing with them huge grapes and figs and pomegranates, which were then just ripe. Among the rest was one cluster of grapes so large that one man could not carry it, and two men had to carry it between them slung on a staff. They shewed the fruits of the land to the people, and said, "The land is a good land, flowing with milk and honey, and full of cornfields and vineyards and olive-orchards, and of fruits like these; but the inhabitants are very strong and fierce; they live in great walled cities, and there are giants among them before whom we seemed in our own sight like grasshoppers, so that our hearts failed us for fear." Ten of the twelve spies said this, and frightened the people; but the other two, Joshua and Caleb, encouraged the people, and told them they need not be afraid.

CHAPTER LXIV
THE MURMURING IN THE WILDERNESS

THEN the people forgot all the great deeds that God had done for them, and the whole camp was full of weeping and murmuring against Moses and Aaron, and saying, "Would God that we had died in the land of Egypt! or would God we had died in this wilderness! were it not better for us to return to Egypt?" From that they broke into open rebellion, and were beginning to choose a captain to lead them back to Egypt, when the glory of God shone out at the door of the tabernacle, and the voice of God spoke, saying that for their disobedience they should wander for forty years in the wilderness until they died there, and their children should enter into their inheritance, and that no one of the grown men among them, except Joshua and Caleb only, should ever see the promised land. The next day the pillar of the cloud and fire rose and turned, and led them back into the wilderness by the way of the Red Sea.

CHAPTER LXV
AARON'S ROD

WHEN the children of Israel returned into the wilderness, three of their princes, called Korah, Dathan, and Abiram, made a mutiny against Moses and Aaron, saying that they had deceived the people with promises of a land flowing with milk and honey, and now, because they could not keep their promise, meant to kill the people in the desert. But the glory shone out at the door of the tabernacle, and Moses bade all the people stand away; and as Korah, Dathan, and Abiram stood by their tents, the ground cleft asunder below them and the earth opened her mouth and swallowed them alive. Thereafter each of the princes of Israel took his rod and laid it in the tabernacle, and Aaron's rod was laid among them. They were left there all night; and in the morning, when they were taken out, the rest of the rods were not changed, but Aaron's rod had budded and blossomed with almond-flowers and bore almonds.

CHAPTER LXVI
THE SERPENT OF BRASS

WHILE the people wandered in the wilderness as the cloud and fire led them, the time came for Aaron to die; and he went up to the top of a mountain, and there Moses took off his holy robes, and put them on Eleazer, Aaron's son; for his other two sons, Nadab and Abihu, had died before this, when they offered strange fire to the Lord in the wilderness; and Aaron died there on the mountain, and Moses and Eleazer came down again to the people. Afterwards they set out on their journey again, and the people were discouraged, and murmured against God. Then he sent fiery serpents into the camp, who bit them, so that many of them died; and they repented and came to Moses, praying him to take the serpents away. Moses made a serpent of brass and set it up on a pole in the camp, and any one who was bitten had only to look at it, and he was cured at once. This serpent of brass was laid up among the treasures of the people for a long while afterwards, till at last one of their kings broke it in pieces.

CHAPTER LXVII
THE VICTORIES IN THE WILDERNESS

WHEN the forty years of the wandering in the wilderness were over, all the people who had been grown men when they left Egypt were dead, except Moses and Joshua and Caleb, and the new generation of their children set out again towards the land of Canaan. On their way, they came down the valley of Arnon to the border of the Amorites; and they sent messengers to Sihon king of the Amorites asking for passage through his land; and promising not to hurt the fields or vineyards, or even to take water from the wells without paying for it, but to go along peaceably by the king's highway till they had passed through.

But king Sihon refused, and came out into the wilderness with all his people to fight against them. They fought at Jahaz, and the children of Israel conquered him and took all his cities. When Sihon's neighbour, Og king of Bashan, heard of this, he armed his people also, and went out to fight with the children of Israel at Edrei. He was one of the giants who were still left on the earth, and was twice as tall as common men, and had a bedstead of iron. But the children of Israel overcame him and his army in battle, and took the sixty walled cities in his kingdom, and possessed his land. Thus they became masters of all the country up to the river Jordan; and they encamped in the plains of Moab near the river, waiting their time to cross over; and from their camp they could see the towers and palm-trees of the city of Jericho opposite them.

CHAPTER LXVIII
BALAAM'S ASS

WHEN Balak king of Moab saw what had befallen the two kings who had fought against Israel, he was afraid to meet them in battle; but he sent to a great magician called

Balaam, who lived in the mountains of the east, to come and curse Israel for him and drive them out of his land. The king's messengers rode into the east till they came to Balaam's house, which stood by a river in the mountains. He lodged them for the night, and the next morning saddled his ass and set out to go back with them. As he rode along a narrow lane among the vineyards with a wall on each side, he met an angel, who was standing in the path with his drawn sword in his hand. Balaam did not see the angel; but the ass saw him, and swerved aside; and when Balaam struck her with his staff to make her go on, she thrust herself to the wall and crushed Balaam's foot against it. He struck her again and made her go past on the other side. But the angel went back a little and stood in a narrow place of the path where there was no room to pass on right or left; and when the ass came up and saw him, she fell down on the path under her master. Balaam, who still did not see the angel, grew very angry, and struck her a third time. Then the ass opened her mouth and said, "What have I done, that you have struck me these three times?" Balaam said, "You have made a fool of me; I wish I had a sword, that I might kill you." She answered, "You have ridden on me ever since I was yours until to-day; have I ever done so to you before?" "No," he said; and his eyes were suddenly opened, and he saw the angel with his drawn sword standing in the path, and fell down on his face before him. Then the angel rebuked Balaam for striking the ass, "For your journey is evil in my eyes," he said; "and if she had not turned out of the way, I would have slain you and saved her alive." Balaam said, "I did not know, my lord; if it displease you, I will go back." The angel answered, "You may go on now; but you must only speak what God shall put in your mouth to say." So they all went on; and the king of Moab went out to his border to meet Balaam, and brought him home to the royal city. The next morning, the king took Balaam up to a mountain-top from which they looked down on the camp of Israel. It lay in the plain by the river below them, and the long rows of tents were like avenues of trees planted by the water; and the king pointed to it and said to Balaam, "Curse Israel for me." Then the Spirit of God came upon Balaam; he fell into a trance with his eyes open, and saw the vision of God; and instead of cursing Israel he blessed them, and foretold that they should grow greater and greater, and that out of them should arise a Star and a Sceptre against which no enchantments could prevail. So the king of Moab sent Balaam away in great anger, and he returned to his own land. But afterwards the Spirit of God left him, and he went with the tribes of the eastern desert to fight against Israel, and was killed in battle.

CHAPTER LXIX
THE HIDDEN GRAVE

GOD said to Moses in the plain of Moab by Jordan, "The time is come for you to die; you shall not live to see the entry into the promised land, or to go over Jordan: only from the top of the mountains of Abarim I will shew you the land afar off." So Moses gathered the people together, and gave them his last counsel, and blessed them, and appointed Joshua the son of Nun to be captain of the people after him, and to lead them into the land of Canaan. Then he went up alone to the mountain-top, and from there God shewed him all the length and breadth of the land, hill and valley and plain, the fields and the cities, from Mount Lebanon to the southern desert, and from the river to the great sea. When he had looked his fill, the glory of God descended upon him and kissed him, and the kiss of God drew his spirit up to Paradise; but his body was buried by the four archangels in a valley under the mountain, where until this day no man knows the place of his grave. He was a hundred and twenty years old when he died, yet his eye was not dimmed nor his strength abated; and no such prophet ever arose after him; and all the children of Israel mourned for him thirty days.

CHAPTER LXX
THE SCARLET RIBBON

WHEN the mourning for Moses was finished, Joshua prepared to go over Jordan; but first of all he sent two men across to spy out the land secretly. They crossed the river and came at evening to the city of Jericho, which lay opposite the camp of the children of Israel; and they looked over the town, and lodged with a woman called Rahab, who had a house on the town wall. But some one saw them in the city, and brought word to the king of Jericho, who sent men to Rahab's house at night to seize them and kill them. Rahab took the spies up to the flat roof of the house and hid them under a heap of flax that was spread out there to dry; and when the king's men came and asked for them she said, "There were two men here, but they left when it grew dark, about the time of shutting the city gate for the night; if you make haste after them you will overtake them." The king's men went off in haste to set guards at the fords of the river, and the town gates were shut after them as they went out, that if the spies were still in the city, they might not be able to escape. But Rahab went up to the spies and told them how she had saved their lives, and took an oath from them in the name of their whole people to spare her and all her family if the children of Israel took the city. They swore to this; then she let them down by a rope from one of her windows on the town wall, bidding them hide among the hills for three days till the guards were taken off the fords; and they gave her a scarlet ribbon and told her to tie it in her window, that her house might be known and no harm come to it when the city were taken. Then they stole off to the hills in the darkness, and hid there till the search for them had been given up; and then they crossed the river again and returned to Joshua and told him what they had seen and heard in Jericho.

CHAPTER LXXI
THE CROSSING OF JORDAN

THEN the children of Israel broke up their camp and marched down to the river, and in front of them the priests went carrying the ark of God. The river was in high flood and over all its banks. But as soon as the priests carrying the ark came to it and their feet touched the edge, the water above them stood still and rose up in a heap, and the water below flowed away, and a dry passage was left, on which all the people crossed over. The priests stood with the ark in the middle of the river-bed till all had passed; then they came up out of the river, and as soon as they reached the other side the waters returned to their channel and filled and overflowed all their banks as before. Joshua picked out twelve men to take twelve great stones from the place in the river-bed where the priests had stood with the ark, and the stones were carried up and laid on the bank for a memorial, that when in times to come children asked, "What do these twelve stones mean?" their fathers might tell them, "It was here that the waters of Jordan were cut off before the ark of the Lord when it passed over." The next morning, the manna on which the children of Israel had fed for forty years in the wilderness ceased; and they fed on the corn and fruits of the land; for it was harvest time. But one pot of manna was kept in the tabernacle, that there might be a memory of the angels' bread with which God had fed his people in the wilderness.

CHAPTER LXXII
THE WALLS OF JERICHO

THE children of Israel encamped all round Jericho, so that no man could go out or in, and besieged it; but the king of Jericho barred the gates, and thought he was safe within the great stone wall of his city. As Joshua was setting the army in array, he saw an angel standing near him with a drawn sword in his hand. He went up and asked him, "Are you for us, or for our adversaries?" and the angel answered, "I am captain of the Lord's host." Joshua fell on his face before him, saying, "What saith my lord to his servant?" and the angel told him what he must do to take the city. Then Joshua gave orders accordingly; and the children of Israel marched round the city with the ark in the middle of the host, and in front of the ark seven priests blowing on seven trumpets of rams' horns; but the people did not shout, or make any noise. The next day they marched round Jericho again in the same manner, and so every day for six days. On the seventh day they rose early and marched round the city seven times; and at the seventh time the priests blew a long blast on their trumpets, and all the host shouted a great shout; and with that shout the wall of the city fell down flat, and the army of Israel went up into Jericho, every man straight before him, and took it, and destroyed it utterly. But the two spies went to the house of Rahab, where the scarlet ribbon was fastened in the window, and brought her away in safety to the camp with her family and all she had.

CHAPTER LXXIII
THE AMBASSADORS

AFTER the taking of Jericho, great fear fell upon all the kings and cities of the land of Canaan, and some of them sent to submit themselves to Joshua, while others prepared to fight against him. But the people of Gibeon persuaded the children of Israel to make peace with them by this device. They took old sacks on their asses, and old wine bottles split and sewn up, and old clothes, and old patched shoes on their feet, and dry mouldy bread, and came to the camp of Israel, saying, "We are ambassadors from a very far country, who have heard the fame of all that God has done for you in the land of Egypt, and are come to make alliance with you." Then they shewed their old worn shoes and clothes, and their mouldy bread, and said, "These clothes were new, and this bread was hot from the oven when we left home, but they have grown old because of the length of our journey." Then Joshua made alliance with them. But a day or two after, he found that they lived in one of the cities of Canaan, quite close by; and he could not touch them, because he had sworn peace with them; but for their deceit they were set to hew wood and draw water for the people.

CHAPTER LXXIV
THE STAYING OF THE SUN AND MOON

WHEN the five kings of the Amorites who dwelt in the hill country of the south heard that the Gibeonites had made peace with Joshua, they gathered a great army and besieged Gibeon. The Gibeonites sent messengers to Joshua to come quickly and help them; and he set out at once and marched all night, and in the morning fell on the camp of the five kings before Gibeon and routed them and pursued them down the hill to Beth-horon, till it was near sunset. But when he saw the sun going fast down, he cried out in the sight of all Israel, "Sun, stand thou still upon Gibeon; and thou, moon, in the valley of Ajalon." Then the moon stayed from rising in the valley, and the sun stood still over the city towers in the midst of heaven about a whole day, till the children of Israel had quite scattered their enemies. The five kings had hidden in a cave, but were found there and dragged out and hanged. Thereafter Joshua conquered all the highlands and lowlands of the south, and fought with seven kings, and overthrew them one by one; and when all the kings of the north gathered their armies by the waters of Merom, he fell on them there and overthrew them all together; so he conquered the whole land; and it was divided among the twelve tribes of Israel for their inheritance.

CHAPTER LXXV
THE DAYS OF THE JUDGES

THE children of Israel settled in the land of Canaan and lived there by their tribes and families, tilling the ground and pasturing their flocks; they had no king over them, but every man did as was right in his own eyes. Only from time to time the nations about them became powerful and oppressed them; and then judges rose up who delivered them from their oppressors and gave the land rest. Such was Ehud, who delivered them from Eglon king of Moab, when he had overrun the land and possessed the city of palm-trees; and Shamgar the son of Anath, who killed six hundred Philistines at one time with his ox-goad; and Jair, who had thirty sons that rode on thirty ass-colts and had thirty cities on the hills; and Barak, and Gideon, and Jephthah, and Samson, of whom it is told thus.

CHAPTER LXXVI
THE IRON CHARIOTS

KING Jabin and Sisera his captain, who lived in a castle in the forest, oppressed Israel with a great army and nine hundred chariots of iron; so that travellers went through byways, and the highways and villages were left without people. At that time Deborah the wife of Lapidoth was a prophetess in Israel, and sat under a palm tree on a mountain. She sent for Barak the son of Abinoam to come to her out of the north country; and when he came, she said, "The Lord God of Israel commands you, Go and draw toward Mount Tabor with ten thousand men; and he will bring Sisera with his army and his chariots to you to the river Kishon, and deliver them into your hand." Barak answered, "I will go if you will go with me, but not else;" and she said, "Then I will go; but the journey shall not be to your honour, for Sisera shall fall by the hand of a woman." Then they went up together to Mount Tabor with ten thousand men at their feet, and Sisera came out of the forest with his nine hundred chariots of iron, and encamped on the plain below by the river Kishon. There Barak and his ten thousand men rushed down upon them from the mountain, and the stars in their courses fought on the side of Israel with thunder and tempest; the river swelled into a fierce torrent and swept away the iron chariots, and all Sisera's army was scattered like dust.

CHAPTER LXXVII
JAEL'S HAMMER

WHEN Sisera saw his army routed, he alighted from his chariot and fled across the plain on foot and alone till he came to where the tents of Heber the Kenite were pitched by a grove of oaks. The men were all away in the fields; but Jael the wife of Heber came out of her tent to meet him, and bade him take refuge with her. He went in with her into the tent, and she covered him with a cloak, and brought him milk to drink; so being very weary, he fell asleep. Then as he slept, she took a tent-pin and a hammer, and going softly to him, struck the pin through both his temples into the ground, and he died. Soon after, Barak came up in pursuit. Jael went out to him, saying, "Come, and I will shew you the man whom you seek;" and when he went with her into the tent, there Sisera lay dead. But in the castle in the forest Sisera's mother sat long that day looking out at her window over the gate, and cried through the lattice, "Why is his chariot so long in coming?"

CHAPTER LXXVIII
THE OAK IN OPHRAH

AFTER this the land had peace, until the Midianites gathered all the children of the East, and came swarming in like grasshoppers, with their camels and tents, and stripped all the land bare, so that the people hid in the dens and caves of the mountains for shelter, and cried to God to deliver them. Then an angel came down and sat under an oak in Ophrah, where Gideon the son of Joash was threshing wheat by his winepress on the rock, and said to him, "Go forth, and save Israel." Gideon answered him, "O my lord, how shall I save Israel? for my family is poor in Manasseh, and I am the least in my father's house." But the angel said, "I will be with you;" and he stretched out the rod in his hand, and touched the rock, and fire rose up out of it; and with that the angel vanished out of sight. Then the Spirit of God came upon Gideon, and he blew a trumpet and gathered the people of the tribes around him, and encamped by a well on the mountain-side with thirty-two thousand men; but the host of the Midianites lay along in the valley below and were like the sand by the sea-side for multitude.

CHAPTER LXXIX
GIDEON'S FLEECE

GIDEON prayed to God to grant him a sign that he was to save Israel; and the sign he asked for was this: that if he left a fleece of wool on the threshing-floor all night, there should be dew on the fleece only, and all the rest of the ground be dry. In the morning it was so; for when he rose early, all the ground was dry, but the fleece was wringing wet, and when he squeezed it together, he wrung a bowlful of water out of it. Then he prayed for another sign, that it might be dry on the fleece and wet on all the ground; and God gave him this also, for the next morning the ground was all wet with dew, and only the fleece was dry.

CHAPTER LXXX
THE CHOOSING OF THE THREE HUNDRED

THEN the word of God came to Gideon, saying, "The people with you are too many; they might boast afterwards that their own strength had won them victory. Proclaim through the army that all who are afraid may go home." So he made proclamation; and twenty-two thousand of his men left him, and ten thousand remained. But God said again, "Still there are too many." Then Gideon brought his ten thousand men down to the water to drink, and three hundred of them lapped the water in the hollow of their hand, and all the rest went down on their knees to drink; and he sent all the rest away, and only kept the three hundred who lapped the water in the hollow of their hand. When Gideon was left with only three hundred men he began to be afraid; but God told him to go down into the valley when it grew dark and listen to what he should hear in the Midianite camp. At nightfall he crept down the hill, and when he got close to the camp he heard one of the soldiers who had just waked out of a dream, telling it to his fellow: "I dreamed," he said, "that a cake of barley bread tumbled into the camp and struck a tent and overturned it, so that the tent lay flat along." When his fellow heard the dream he answered, "This is nothing else but the sword of Gideon the son of Joash, a man of Israel; for God has delivered Midian and all our host into his hand."

CHAPTER LXXXI
THE TRUMPETS AT MIDNIGHT

WHEN Gideon heard this he climbed up again to his own camp, and divided his three hundred men into three companies, giving every man a trumpet and an empty jar with a lighted lamp in it, and ordered them to spread out silently round the enemy's camp; and when he gave the signal by blowing his trumpet, all to blow their trumpets together on every side of the camp, and cry, "The sword of the Lord and of Gideon." So they went silently down and surrounded the camp at midnight, just after the middle watch was set; and at the signal they all broke their jars and held up their lamps in one hand, and with the other they held their trumpets and blew, and cried, "The sword of the Lord and of Gideon." The Midianite army were startled out of sleep, and rose and cried and fled, and in the darkness they all turned their swords against each other, till a hundred and twenty thousand men that drew sword lay dead on the ground.

CHAPTER LXXXII
THE CHASE OF THE KINGS

ALL next day Gideon and his three hundred men pursued the two kings of Midian, who had fled across Jordan into the desert with about fifteen thousand men that were left of their army. As he passed through the cities of Succoth and Penuel he asked for bread, for he had brought no food with him, and his men were faint with hunger. But the townspeople refused it, saying,

"Are the hands of the kings of Midian in your hand, that we should give you bread?" Gideon did not stop then, but followed the track across the desert, and falling on the Midianite camp by night, he scattered them and took both their kings prisoners. Before the sun was up he returned upon Succoth and Penuel, and shewed them the captive kings: then he took thorns and briars of the wilderness, and with them he taught the men of Succoth, and he beat down the tower of Penuel and slew the men of the city. When he returned home from the chase of the kings, the people came to him and asked him to be king over them, because he had delivered them from the hand of Midian. But he would not, and went back to live in his own house, and died there in a good old age; and for forty years more the land had peace.

CHAPTER LXXXIII
THE STORY OF THE TREES WHO WENT OUT TO CHOOSE A KING

WHEN Gideon died he left seventy sons (for he had many wives) and also one son called Abimelech, whose mother was a woman of the city of Shechem. After his father's death Abimelech went to Shechem to his mother's family and made friends with the people of the town, who gave him money out of their treasury. With this money he hired a band of broken men and went to his father's house, and there killed his seventy brothers upon one stone, all except the youngest, called Jotham, who hid himself and escaped. Then the men of Shechem assembled and made Abimelech king. But Jotham went to the top of the hill above Shechem and there stood and cried to the people of the town: " Hear me, men of Shechem, that God may hear you. Once upon a time, the trees went forth to choose a king ; and they said to the olive-tree, Reign over us. But the olive-tree said to them, Should I leave my fatness, wherewith by me they honour God and man, and go to be promoted over the trees? Then the trees said to the fig-tree, Come you, and reign over us. But the fig-tree said to them, Should I forsake my sweetness and my good fruit, and go to be promoted over the trees? Then the trees said to the vine, Come you, and reign over us. But the vine said to them, Should I leave my wine, which cheers God and man, and go to be promoted over the trees? Then all the trees said to the bramble: Come you, and reign over us. And the bramble said to the trees, If you choose me truly to be king over you, then come and put your trust in my shadow; and if not, let fire come out of the bramble and devour the cedars of Lebanon. Now look to it, O men of Shechem, whether you have done well by my father's house. My father fought for you, and adventured his life far, and delivered you out of the hand of Midian; and you have risen up against my father's house to-day, and have slain his sons, threescore and ten persons, upon one stone, and have made Abimelech, the son of his maidservant, king. If you have dealt truly with my father's house to-day, then rejoice in Abimelech and let him also rejoice in you; but if not, let fire come out from each of you and destroy the other."

CHAPTER LXXXIV
THE TOWER OF THISBE

WHEN Jotham had spoken thus from the hill, he ran away and hid himself, and Abimelech reigned over Israel. But soon the men of Shechem quarrelled with him, and when he was away, they began to fortify their city against him; and the men of the city of Thisbe joined them, and did likewise. Then the captain whom Abimelech had left in Shechem sent to him secretly, bidding him come by night and lie in wait outside the city in four companies, and set upon it in the morning as soon as the sun was up. About sunrise next morning, the captain of the men of Shechem stood in the city gate, and saw one of the companies that were lying in wait moving down from the hill. He said to Abimelech's captain, who was standing beside him, "Who are those yonder?" and he laughed, and answered, "You see the shadows of the hills as if they were men." But presently more bands of men began to appear, coming by the middle of the plain and past the Wizards' Oak; then the men of Shechem armed hastily and went out to battle; and they were beaten and chased back into the city. They gathered to make a stand in the tower of their temple; but Abimelech sent men to cut boughs from the forest, and heaped them round the tower and set them on fire, and burned the tower and all the people in it. Then Abimelech marched against the city of Thisbe and took it, driving the men of the city into their tower like the men of Shechem. But as he came up to the tower to set fire to the door, a woman on the top of the tower threw down a millstone on him which struck him on the head and killed him; and so the curse of Jotham came on Abimelech, and on the men of Shechem.

CHAPTER LXXXV
JEPHTHAH'S DAUGHTER

AFTERWARDS the children of Ammon oppressed Israel. They conquered the tribes that lived beyond Jordan in Gilead, and crossed over Jordan to make war against the other tribes; and the children of Israel gathered to fight with them and encamped in Mizpeh; but they had no captain to lead them. Now there was a mighty man then called Jephthah, whom his brothers had thrust out of his inheritance after their father's death, because he was the son of a strange woman; and he had gone to a foreign country and become a great captain; so the elders of the people sent for him, and made him judge over Israel to lead them in battle against the children of Ammon. Jephthah came to the camp at Mizpeh, and sent messengers to the king of Ammon bidding him go back into his own country; but he would not, and so the two armies prepared for battle. Before they met, Jephthah made a vow that if he conquered the enemy he would offer in sacrifice whatever first came out of the door of his house to meet him on his return. Then he joined battle, and smote the children of Ammon with great slaughter from Aroer to Minnith, and took twenty of their cities. But when he returned from the battle to his house at Mizpeh, his daughter, who was his only child, came out to welcome him, dancing to music; and when he saw her, he rent his clothes, and cried out, "Alas! my daughter." But she said, "Let me die, since my people have taken vengeance on the children of Ammon; only let me go up and down on the mountains for two months with my companions to bewail myself."

So she went to the mountains with her companions, and at the end of two months she returned to her father, and he did with her according to his vow.

CHAPTER LXXXVI
THE LION IN THE VINEYARDS

AFTERWARDS the children of Israel were oppressed by the Philistines: and an angel appeared to a woman of Israel, the wife of Manoah of Zorah, and told her that she should bear a son who would deliver the people. She told this to her husband, and he prayed to God: "O Lord, let thine angel come again to us to tell us how we shall bring up the child who shall be born." Then the angel came again and told them what they were to do, and that the child's hair was never to be cut, for his strength would be in it, and by his strength he would do great deeds. Then Manoah offered sacrifice upon a rock, and when the flame went up from the sacrifice, the angel went up into heaven with the flame. Afterwards they had a son born, whom they called Samson; as he grew up he became stronger than all other men; and his strength lay in his long uncut hair. On a day, as he was going through the vineyards, a lion roared at him; he had no weapon in his hand, but he sprang on the lion and tore him with his naked hands as if he had been a kid, and then went on his way and said nothing about it. After a while he was going to be married at Timnath and passed by the place where he had killed the lion. He turned aside to look at the dead lion, and found that a swarm of bees had made their honey in the dry carcase; and he took out a piece of the honeycomb and ate it as he went along.

CHAPTER LXXXVII
SAMSON'S RIDDLE

WHEN Samson came to Timnath, the marriage feast was made, and thirty of his companions were there as guests. At the feast they asked riddles; and Samson said to his companions, "I will ask you a riddle, and if you can tell me the answer before the seven days of the feast are over, I will give each of you a sheet and a change of garments; but if you cannot guess it, you shall give me thirty sheets and thirty changes of garments." They all said,

"Put forth your riddle." Then he said, "Out of the eater came forth meat, and out of the strong came forth sweetness." They could not guess the riddle; and at last when it was the seventh day they went to the bride and said to her, "You must make Samson tell you the answer, and let us know it, or we will burn your father's house." She went to Samson and burst into tears, saying, "You do not love me if you will not tell me the answer to your riddle." For a while he would not tell her, but at last she wearied him into telling her; then she went away and told his thirty companions, and just before sunset they came to Samson, and said, "What is sweeter than honey? and what is stronger than a lion?" He answered, "If you had not ploughed with my heifer, you would not have found out my riddle;" and went away to the country of the Philistines, who were at war with Israel, and there killed thirty men in battle and brought back their garments, and gave them to his companions; then he broke off his marriage, and went back in anger to his father's house; but the bride was given in marriage to one of his thirty companions.

CHAPTER LXXXVIII
THE GATES OF GAZA

SAMSON had set fire to the standing corn of the Philistines and gone to live on the top of a rock; and the Philistines sent out armed men to take him. The men of Judah promised to give him up, if the Philistines would make peace with them; so they climbed up the rock and found him there, and said to him, " What is this you have done to the Philistines?" He said, "I have only done to them as they have done to me." They said, "We have come to bind you and give you up to them." He answered, "Very well; only swear to me that you will not kill me yourselves." They swore to this, and then he let them disarm him and bind him with two new cords, and bring him down from the rock. But when he came to the Philistines, he snapped the cords like threads of flax, and caught up the jawbone of an ass that lay on the ground and killed a thousand Philistines with it. Then he went to the city of Gaza, and the men of the city, when they knew that he was there, barred their gates and kept quiet all night, intending to search for him and kill him as soon as it was daylight. But at midnight he rose and went to the gate, and finding it locked, he wrenched the gates off, with the gate-posts and bar, and went away carrying them on his shoulder, and left them on the top of a hill outside the city on the road to Hebron.

CHAPTER LXXXIX
THE STOLEN SECRET

AFTERWARDS Samson loved a woman called Delilah, who lived in the valley of the vineyards; and the five lords of the Philistines bribed her with eleven hundred pieces of silver to entice him to tell her the secret of his great strength, that they might take him. So she asked him, and he told her: "If I were bound with seven green withies that were never dried, my strength would leave me." Then the lords of the Philistines brought her seven green withies and set men to lie in wait in the chamber; and she bound him while he slept, and cried, "The Philistines are upon you, Samson." At the cry he started up, and the withies broke like a thread when it touches the fire; so the secret of his strength was not known. Then Delilah said to him, "You have mocked me and told me lies; tell me now truly with what you may be bound;" and he said, "If they bind me with new ropes that have never been used, I shall be weak like another man." So the Philistines set men to lie in wait again, and she bound him with new ropes, and cried out, "The Philistines are upon you, Samson." But he rose and broke the ropes off his arms like a thread. Then she asked him again to tell her truly; and he told her to weave the seven locks of his hair into the web on the loom. But when she did so as he lay asleep, and cried out to him, he awoke and tore the pin out of the beam and went away carrying the web. At last she said to him, "How can you say you love me, when you will not tell me your secret, and have mocked me and told me lies three times?" and she wearied him and gave him no peace day after day, till at last he told her the truth, that if his hair were cut off, he would become as weak as any other man. Then Delilah sent for the lords of the Philistines to come once more; and they came with the money in their hands and set armed men to lie in wait in the chamber. While Samson was asleep with his head in her lap, a man came in and shaved off the seven locks of his head, and his strength went from him. Then Delilah cried out, "The Philistines are upon you, Samson;" and he awoke and did not know what had been done to him, but said, "I will go out as before and shake myself." But the Philistines took him easily, and put out his eyes and brought him to their city of Gaza; and there they bound him in fetters of brass and set him to grind corn in the prison. But when he was in prison his hair began to grow again, and his strength to come back with it.

CHAPTER XC
SAMSON'S REVENGE

THE lords and people of the Philistines assembled at Gaza to hold a great festival and rejoice over Samson; and when they had feasted, they sent for Samson out of prison to make sport for them. A boy led him from the prison into the great hall where all the lords and ladies sat below, and crowds of the common people were outside on the roof looking on. When Samson had made sport for them, he said to the boy that led him, "Let me lean on the pillars that bear up the house, and rest for a little." The boy guided him to the pillars and set him between them; and when he felt them in his hands he called to God, and said, "O Lord God, remember me, I pray thee, and strengthen me, I pray thee, only this once, O God, that I may be avenged of the Philistines for my two eyes." Then he took hold of the two pillars with his two hands, and crying out, "Let me die with the Philistines," he bowed himself with all his might and tore the pillars away, and the house fell in upon himself and the lords and the people, and crushed them all to death; so the dead whom Samson slew at his death were more than all those whom he had slain in his life.

CHAPTER XCI
THE FAMINE AT BETHLEHEM

IN the days of the Judges there was a famine in the land of Israel; and a man of Bethlehem in Judah, with his wife Naomi and their two sons, because food was scarce at home, left his plot of land there and went to live in the country of Moab. There he died, and his two sons married two women of Moab called Orpah and Ruth. When they had lived there for about ten years, the two sons both died also, one after the other; and Naomi set out to return to her own land again; for she had heard that God had visited his people, and given them abundance of bread.

CHAPTER XCII
THE VOW OF RUTH

NAOMI'S two daughters-in-law set forth with her on her journey; and when they were gone a little way, Naomi bade them turn and go back, saying to them, "Go, return each of you to her mother's house; may the Lord deal kindly with you, as you have dealt with the dead and with me; may the Lord grant you to find rest, each of you in the house of her husband." Then she kissed them, and they wept and said to her, "Surely we will return with you to your people." But she answered, "Turn again, my daughters; for I can do nothing more for you; it grieves me most for your sake that the hand of the Lord is heavy on me." Then they wept again, and Orpah kissed her and returned home. But Ruth clung to her and said, "Entreat me not to leave you, or to return from following you; for whither you go I will go, and where you lodge I will lodge; your people shall be my people and your God my God; where you die will I die, and there will I be buried; may God forget me if anything but death shall ever part you and me." When Naomi saw that Ruth was fixed in her purpose, she said no more, and they went on together until they came to Bethlehem.

CHAPTER XCIII
THE GLEANER

BARLEY harvest was beginning at Bethlehem; and Ruth said to her mother-in-law, "Let me go into the fields and glean corn, wherever they will allow me;" and Naomi said, "Go, my daughter." So she went and gleaned in the fields after the reapers; and as it chanced, she lighted on a field belonging to a rich man called Boaz, a kinsman of Naomi's husband. While she gleaned behind the reapers, Boaz came out from Bethlehem, and gave greeting to his harvesters, saying, "The Lord be with you;" and they answering, "The Lord bless you." When he saw Ruth among the gleaners, he said to the servant who was in charge of his reapers, "Whose girl is that?" and he answered, "It is the woman of Moab that has come back with Naomi out of the country of Moab; she asked leave to glean after the reapers among the sheaves, and she has been at work from morning till now." Then Boaz went up to Ruth and said to her, "Do you hear, my child? do not go to glean in another field, but keep here by my maidens; I have told the young men not to annoy you; and when you are thirsty, go to the vessels, and drink of what has been drawn for the harvesters. I have heard of your goodness to your mother-in-law ever since your husband died, and how you left your own land and kin to come here with her: may a full reward be given you by the Lord God of Israel, under whose wings you are come to trust." Ruth thanked him and bowed to the ground before him, and so she gleaned in his barley field all morning. When dinner-time came, he told her to sit among the reapers and eat and drink with them. Then she rose up to glean again; and Boaz told his men to let her glean as close among the sheaves as she would, and to let fall some of the handfuls on purpose and leave them for her. So she was busy in the field till evening, and then beat out what she had gleaned. This came to about three measures of barley, which she took up and carried home into the town, and she told Naomi of her day's work, and the name of the man in whose field she had gleaned. Then Naomi said, "God bless him, because he has not failed in kindness to the living and the dead; he is one of our nearest kinsmen." "He told me," said Ruth, "to keep by his men till they had ended their harvest;" and Naomi said, "It is good, my daughter; go out with his maidens, and do not be found in any other field." So Ruth gleaned every day among the maidens of Boaz till the end of the harvest.

CHAPTER XCIV
THE THRESHING-FLOOR IN THE DARK

THEN Naomi said to Ruth, "My daughter, shall I not seek rest for you, that it may be well with you? Boaz our kinsman is winnowing barley to-night on his threshing-floor; go there at nightfall, and after he has supped and lain down to sleep, go and lie down at his feet and for the rest, do as he tells you." So Ruth washed and dressed herself, and went out at nightfall to the winnowing-floor. When it grew dark, Boaz ate his supper, and went to lie down at the end of the heap of winnowed corn, and she came softly and lay at his feet. In the middle of the night he awoke and turned himself, and felt a woman lying at his feet. He said, "Who are you?" and she said, "I am Ruth your servant; spread your skirt over me, for you are my near kinsman." He answered, "God bless you, my child, for coming to me and not going after young men, whether they were poor or rich. But there is a nearer kinsman than I; if he will do his part, it is well; and if not, I will; lie down till morning." In the grey of the morning he awoke her and made her hold her cloak, and measured six measures of barley into it and sent her home. Then Ruth told Naomi what had happened, and she said to her, "Sit still, my daughter, till you know how things will befal; for the man will not be at rest till he have finished the matter this day."

CHAPTER XCV
THE KINSMEN

WHEN day broke Boaz went up from his threshing-floor to the city and sat down in the city gate, and presently the kinsman of whom he had spoken to Ruth came by; to whom he said, " Ho, such a one! turn aside and sit down here;" and he called ten of the elders of the city, and they all sat down together in the gate. Then Boaz said to his kinsman, " Naomi has come back from the country of Moab, and has a plot of land to sell which belonged to her husband; if you will buy it, let me know, for I am next of kin after you." The kinsman said, " I am willing to buy it." Then Boaz said, " Whoever buys the land must also take with it Ruth the Moabitess, her son's widow, to keep up the name of the dead upon his inheritance." The kinsman said, " I cannot do that; do you buy the land and take the woman." Then Boaz said to the elders and the people in the gate, " Bear witness that I have bought the plot of land from Naomi; and that with it I take Ruth to be my wife, that the name of the dead may not be cut off from among his brethren." So Boaz married Ruth; and they had a child, whom Naomi laid in her bosom and nursed; and the women said to her, "This child shall be a new life to you; for your daughter-in-law, who is better to you than seven sons, has borne him."

CHAPTER XCVI
THE CHILD IN THE TEMPLE

THERE was a man of the hill-country, who had two wives, called Hannah and Peninnah; and he loved Hannah the best, but she had no children, and Peninnah mocked her. Every year he went up to worship and make offerings at Shiloh, the house of God's rest; and when he went, he took his two wives with him. But Hannah fretted sorely because she had no children, and went to the temple, where Eli the high priest sat on the high seat by the doorway, and there she wept and prayed in an agony, so that Eli thought she was a drunken woman and spoke sharply to her. But when she told him how she was in great sorrow and was pouring out her soul before God, he said to her, "Go in peace; and may God grant you your petition that you have asked of him." So they went home to the hill-country; and within a year afterwards Hannah had a son, whom she called Samuel; and when he was weaned, she took him up with her to God's house in Shiloh and brought him to Eli, and said, "My lord, I am the woman that stood here praying to God; for this child I prayed, and God has given him to me; therefore he shall be given to the service of God for all his life." So the child stayed at Shiloh and served in the temple, being a little child with a linen pinafore; and every year his mother made him a little coat and brought it up with her when she came to see him.

CHAPTER XCVII
THE VOICE BY NIGHT

IN those days the words of God were precious, and he did not show himself openly; for the sons of Eli the high priest were wicked men who brought shame on the temple. Eli was growing old, and his eyes were dim; and Samuel slept at nights in the temple before the ark. One night when Samuel had lain down to sleep, but before the lamp that burned in front of the ark had gone out, a voice called him by his name. He thought that Eli had called him, and cried, "Here I am," and ran to Eli. But Eli said, "I did not call you; lie down again." He went back and lay down; and again a voice called, "Samuel!" He rose a second time and went to Eli; but Eli said, "I did not call you; lie down again;" so he went back to bed. Then once more the voice in the dark temple called, "Samuel!" and when he rose and went to Eli the third time, Eli perceived that God had called the child, and said to him, "Go, lie down; and if the voice calls you again, say, Speak, Lord, for thy servant heareth." So Samuel went and lay down in his place, and God came and stood and called, "Samuel! Samuel!" He answered, "Speak, Lord, for thy servant heareth;" and God said, "Because Eli's sons have given themselves up to wickedness, and he has not restrained them, I will send a judgment on his house which shall make the ears of all who hear of it tingle; and no sacrifice shall purge them; for what I begin, that I end." When God had finished speaking to him, Samuel lay still until morning, and then rose and opened the doors of the temple as he did every morning;

but he was afraid to tell Eli of his vision, until Eli called him and asked him, "What is it that he has said to you?" Then Samuel told him of it all, and hid nothing from him; and he said, "It is the Lord; let him do what seems him good." But when Samuel grew up, God continued with him, and he became a prophet, and his words went through all Israel.

CHAPTER XCVIII
THE ARK IN BATTLE

THE children of Israel fought against the Philistines, and were beaten; therefore they sent for the ark out of Shiloh to come to the army and give them victory. Eli's two sons brought the ark into the camp, and when it came, all the people shouted a great shout, so that the earth rang again. The Philistines heard it and wondered; and when they learned that the ark was come into the camp, they were mightily afraid, and said to one another, "God is come into their camp; woe unto us! who shall deliver us out of the hands of these mighty gods that smote the Egyptians with all the plagues in the wilderness?" Yet they resolved to do their best, saying to one another, "Quit yourselves like men, and fight, O Philistines, that you may not be servants to the men of Israel, as they have been to you." Then they joined battle; and the men of Israel fled, and there was a great slaughter; and the ark was taken by the Philistines, and both Eli's sons were slain. A man ran out of the army and came to Shiloh the same day, with his clothes rent and earth upon his head, telling the news, and a great crying rose. Eli was sitting on a seat by the roadside at the city gate, waiting for news of the ark; he heard the crying, and asked, "What does this noise mean?" The messenger came up to him and said, "I fled to-day out of the army." Eli said, "What has happened there, my son?" He answered, "Israel is fled before the Philistines, and there has been a great slaughter among the people; your two sons also are dead; and the ark of God is taken." When Eli heard of the ark, he fell from off his seat backward by the side of the gate, dead.

CHAPTER XCIX
THE TERROR OF THE ARK

THE Philistines took the ark away with them to their own city of Ashdod, and there they set it in the temple of their god Dagon, and left it there for the night. The next morning when they opened the temple doors Dagon was fallen on his face to the ground before the ark. They took him and set him up in his place again, and left him; but the morning after, he had fallen down on his face again before the ark, and his head and both his hands were broken off and lay upon the threshold. Then the people of Ashdod were afraid, and called a council of the lords of the Philistines, by whose advice the ark was sent away to other cities, first to Gath, and then to Ekron; but in each city where it stayed it brought plague and sickness on the people; and after seven months they were afraid to keep it among them any longer. Then they took counsel of their magicians, who advised them to send back the ark. "Make a new cart," they said, "and take two cows who have never been under the yoke; harness them to the cart, and shut their calves up at home; then take the ark and lay it upon the cart, and put jewels and gold for a trespass-offering in a coffer on the cart beside it, and leave the cows to take their own way. If they go up by the House of the Sun to the border of Israel, then we shall know that it is the ark that has done us this evil; but if they do not, then it is not the God of the ark who has smitten us, but it was all a chance that happened." The Philistines did so; and when the ark was laid on the cart, the cows set off by themselves and took the straight way to the House of the Sun, and went along the highway lowing as they went and not turning aside either to right or left; and the five lords of the Philistines followed the cart as far as the border, watching them. The men of the House of the Sun were reaping their wheat harvest in the valley, when they looked up and saw the ark coming. The cows came into the field and stood still of their own accord by a great stone. The reapers came round and took the ark off the cart, and laid it on the stone; and when the five lords of the Philistines saw this, they went back to Ekron. After this there was peace between Israel and the Philistines; and the people of the City of

Woods sent down to the House of the Sun and fetched the ark up into the hills, and kept it there.

CHAPTER C
THE LOST ASSES

WHEN Samuel grew old, he set his sons to judge the people of Israel; but they took bribes and perverted justice; then all the people gathered together and said to Samuel, "Give us a king to judge us, and to go out before us to battle, like the kings of other nations;" and God said to Samuel, "Do as they ask, and make them a king." In those days there was a man of the tribe of Benjamin called Saul, who was the goodliest of presence among all the children of Israel, and stood higher by the head and shoulders than any of the people. The asses of Saul's father strayed and were lost; and he told Saul to take a servant with him and go to seek them. They went through the land along and across for three days, searching for the asses, until they came to the hill-country of Judah; but they could not find them. At last Saul said to the servant, "Come, let us go home again, or my father will leave off caring for the asses and be anxious about us." The servant answered, "There is a wise man who lives in yonder town on the hill-top, and all that he says comes true; perhaps he might shew us the way we should go." "But we have nothing to give him," said Saul, "even the food we brought with us is all done." The servant said, "I have a small piece of silver with me; I will give it to the wise man to tell us our way." Saul answered, "Well said; come, let us go;" so they went up the hill to the town. As they went up, they met the girls of the town coming out to draw water, and asked them, "Is the wise man here?" They answered, all speaking at once, "Yes, he is in front of you, if you make haste; he has just come to the city to-day, for there is a feast to-day in the high place; if you make haste into the city you will find him at once, before he goes up to the high place to eat; the people will not eat till he comes, because he first blesses the feast, and afterwards those who are invited sit down and eat; go up, and you will find him now." Then Saul and his servant went up, and met the wise man coming out of the gate on his way to the high place. Now this wise man was Samuel; and when he met Saul, God said to him, "This is the man whom I have chosen to be captain over my people Israel."

CHAPTER CI
THE STREET AT DAWN

SAUL came up and asked Samuel where the wise man lived; and Samuel answered, "I am he. Come with me and eat, and to-morrow I will let you go. As for the asses that were lost three days ago, do not be troubled about them, for they are found; and on whom but you is the desire of all Israel?" Then he took Saul with him to the high place, and gave him the chief seat among all the guests; so they feasted, and Samuel took Saul home with him at night. At daybreak the next morning they rose and went out together. No one was stirring in the street; and as they went along Samuel stopped and said to Saul, "Bid the servant pass on before us, and stand still here alone with me." Then he took out a vial of oil and anointed him, saying, "You are the man that shall be king of Israel. When you have left me, you will meet two men by Rachel's grave, who will tell you that the asses you went out to seek have been found. Then you will go on, and come to the oak on the hill, and there you will meet three men, one carrying three kids, another three loaves of bread, and the third a bottle of wine; they will give you greeting and two loaves of bread. Then you will come to the hill of God, and near it you will meet a company of prophets coming down from the high place with harps and flutes, prophesying; and the spirit of God will come upon you, and you will prophesy along with them. Afterwards you must go to the gathering-place of the people, and wait for me there." Then Samuel went back to his house, and Saul went on his way, and everything happened that day as Samuel had foretold him. At the gathering-place of the people his uncle met him and asked him, "Where have you been?" Saul said, "To seek the asses that were lost; and when we did not see them anywhere, we went to Samuel." "What did Samuel say to you?" his uncle asked. Saul said nothing about the kingdom, but only answered, "He told us plainly that the asses were found." Presently Samuel came, and lots were drawn among the people by tribes and families to choose a king. The lot fell on Saul's tribe, and then on his family, and then on himself; and when they fetched him and brought him out before the people, he stood higher than any one else by his head and shoulders. Samuel said, " See you him whom the Lord hath chosen, that there is none like him among all the people?" and all the people shouted, and said, " God save the King!"

CHAPTER CII
THE GAP IN THE CLIFFS

THE Philistines overran the land of Israel with a great army, so that the people hid themselves in caves and thickets and rocks and pits, or went away across Jordan; and Saul could only gather a little army of about six hundred men. He encamped under a pomegranate tree, and the army of the Philistines lay on the hills opposite him, and there was a narrow way up to their camp through a gap in the cliffs. As the armies lay there, Jonathan the son of Saul said to his armour-bearer, "Come, let us go over and attack the Philistines." He answered, "I am with you." Jonathan said, "We will shew ourselves, and if they bid us come up, we will go up, but if they say, Stay there until we come to you, we will stand still." Then they shewed themselves in front of the hill, and the Philistines said to one another, "See, the children of Israel are coming out of the holes where they had hid themselves," and called down to them, "Come up to us, and we will shew you something." Then Jonathan, bidding his armour-bearer follow him, climbed up the rocks on his hands and knees, and attacked them; and the whole of their army was seized with panic and took to flight, beating one another down as they fled. The noise came across the valley to Saul, who gathered his men and started in pursuit; and the people who were hidden in the hills came out of their holes and joined him, and the battle rolled far away. As he started, Saul laid a curse on any one who should taste food or turn aside in the pursuit till nightfall. When it grew towards evening, and they were faint for hunger, the battle passed into a wood where honey dropped from the trees; and no one dared to touch it. But Jonathan, who had not heard the curse, dipped the end of his spear into the honey and ate of it and was strengthened. At nightfall they stopped in the pursuit, and supped in haste, and Saul enquired of the oracle whether he should go on after the enemy all night; but it would not answer. Then Saul said, "Some one has broken the curse; he must die, were it my own son." So they cast lots to find out who it was, and the lot fell on Jonathan. Saul said to him, "What have you done?" and he said, "I did but taste a little honey with the end of the rod that was in my hand, and lo! I must die." But the people all cried out, "Shall Jonathan die, who has wrought this great salvation in Israel? There shall not one hair of his head fall to the ground." So they rescued Jonathan, and Saul stopped from pursuing the Philistines, and both the armies broke up and returned home.

CHAPTER CIII
THE BOY HARPER

FROM time to time an evil spirit troubled King Saul, and his servants sought out a harp-player to come and play before him when the evil spirit troubled him. They found in the town of Bethlehem in Judah a shepherd boy called David, the youngest of the seven sons of Jesse of Bethlehem, who was the grandson of Boaz and Ruth. David was a cunning harp-player; and when the evil spirit came on Saul, he came and played to him until he was well; then he went back to Bethlehem and fed his father's sheep. But his six brothers were all in the army that fought under king Saul.

CHAPTER CIV
THE GIANT'S CHALLENGE

THE Philistines made war again upon the children of Israel; and now they had a great giant in their army called Goliath of Gath. He was eleven feet high, and was all armed in brass, with helmet and mail-coat and gorget and greaves; his coat of mail weighed two hundred and fifty pounds. The two armies lay facing each other in a wooded valley; and every morning and every evening Goliath came out in front of the camp, with his armour-bearer going before him and carrying his shield, and challenged the army of Israel; but no one dared to go out to fight with him. On a day, Jesse said to David, "Go to-morrow to the camp and take your brothers some bread and cheese and parched corn, and see how they all are." Next morning, David rose at the first break of dawn, leaving his sheep with a keeper, and made such good speed that when he reached the camp it was still morning and they were setting the battle in array. Then the giant Goliath came out in front of the army of the Philistines and cried, "I challenge the whole army of Israel; send out a man, that we may fight." David heard the soldiers saying that any one who overcame the giant should have great riches and marry the king's daughter; and he said, "Why does no one go out and fight with him?" His eldest brother heard him, and was very angry. "How have you got here, boy?" he said; "and with whom have you left those few sheep in the wilderness?" "I only asked a question," David answered; and with that he went straight to king Saul, and said to him, "O king, let me go and fight with this Philistine." "You cannot, you are too young," said the king. David answered, "When I was keeping my father's sheep, a lion and a bear came and took a lamb out of the flock. I went out after them and pulled the lamb out of the lion's mouth; and when he turned on me, I caught him by the mane and killed him, and then I killed the bear too; and God, who saved me from the paw of the lion and the paw of the bear, will save me from the hand of this Philistine."

CHAPTER CV
THE FIVE SMOOTH STONES

THEN King Saul gave David leave to go forth and fight, and offered him his own armour to wear; but when David put it on and tried to go in it, it was not easy, for he had never worn armour before; so he took it all off again, and picked five smooth pebbles out of the brook and put them in his shepherd's scrip, and took his sling in his hand and went out against Goliath. The giant came on, with his armour-bearer carrying his shield before him, and when he saw an unarmed boy coming to meet him, he broke into a rage, and cursed him by his gods. But David took a stone out of his scrip and laid it in his sling, and ran towards Goliath and slung it. It struck him on his forehead under the rim of the helmet, and he fell forward on his face stunned; then David ran lightly up and drew Goliath's sword out of the sheath as he lay, and cut off his head at a blow. When the Philistines saw their champion fallen, they all fled, and David brought back the giant's head and his armour to the camp. So he was married to Saul's daughter

Michal, and was made commander of the army; and Jonathan, Saul's son, loved him like his own brother.

CHAPTER CVI
THE IMAGE UNDER THE COUNTERPANE

BUT when Saul and David came back together, the women went out to meet them dancing and singing, "Saul has slain his thousands, and David his ten thousands." Saul grew very angry, and thought, "They have ascribed to David ten thousands, and to me only thousands, and what can he have more but the kingdom?" and from that day forth he hated David. The next day the evil spirit came on him; and when David went in to play to him as he sat alone, he threw a javelin at him; but David slipped aside, and the javelin flew past him and stuck into the wall. David ran away home, and Saul sent men to keep watch at his door all night and kill him when he came out in the morning; but at night his wife Michal let him down through a window, and he fled away. In the morning Saul sent more men to fetch David; then she took an image and laid it in David's bed, with its head on the pillow, and drew the counterpane over it, and told them that David was ill. They went back to Saul, who sent them again, saying, "Bring him to me in the bed, that I may kill him." So they went into the bedroom, and when they pulled away the counterpane, they found nothing but an image in the bed. But David went to the temple at the high place where the sword of Goliath was laid up behind the altar-screen, and he took the sword and went into the mountains, where he and a band of his followers lived in caves in the forest.

CHAPTER CVII
THE CAMP IN THE FOREST

SAUL was told where David lay in hiding in the wilderness, and he and his chief captain Abner went with three thousand men to seek him out. David withdrew further into the mountains, leaving watchmen to let him know when Saul's men came. So they searched the forest all day without finding him, and then encamped on the hill for the night. But in the middle of the night, David and his sister's son Abishai crept in softly to Saul's camp, and found every one asleep, and Saul asleep among them with his spear stuck in the ground by his pillow and a jug of water at his head. Abishai whispered to David, "God has delivered your enemy into your hand; let me run him through with the spear, and I will not strike a second time." David answered, "No; his day shall come to die, or he shall go into battle and perish; but God forbid that I should stretch forth my hand against the Lord's anointed. Take the spear that is by his pillow, and the water-jug, and let us go." So they took the jug and the spear, and stole out of the camp again silently without awaking anyone. They climbed down into the bed of the torrent at the foot of the hill and up the other side, until at daybreak they were opposite the camp with the deep narrow valley between; then David stood and shouted across, "Answer you not, Abner?" Abner awoke and answered, "Who are you that cry to the king?" Then David cried across the valley in the clear dawn, "Are you not a valiant man? why have you not kept watch over your lord the king? for there came one of the people in to kill him. By God's life, you deserve to be put to death for keeping your master so ill. See where the king's spear is now, and the jug of water that stood at his pillow."

So when Saul knew that David might easily have killed him, and had spared his life, he said he would do him no more harm, and returned home; and David and his men came back and lived again in the forest.

CHAPTER CVIII
THE WITCH OF ENDOR

SAMUEL was dead, and Saul's kingdom was failing in his hands, and the Philistines made war on him again with a great army. Saul was afraid, and sought to use divinations, and find out how the battle would go; but he could get no answer from dreams, or precious stones, or prophets. Then he told his servants to find out a witch, that he might enquire of her. This was not easy, because Saul had put away all the witches from his land; but at last they found a woman with a familiar spirit at Endor. Saul disguised himself, and went with two servants at dead of night to her house, and said to her, "Divine to me by the familiar spirit, and bring up to me him whom I shall name." The witch answered, "You know that King Saul has put away all the wizards and those who have familiar spirits out of the land; are you laying a trap for my life?" He swore that no harm should befal her; then she asked, "Whom shall I bring up for you?" "Bring me up Samuel," he said. Suddenly the witch shrieked aloud and cried, "Why have you deceived me? you are Saul." "Do not be afraid," said the king; "whom did you see?" She said, "I saw a spirit ascending out of the earth." "What form is he of?" said the king. She answered, "An old man comes up, covered with a mantle." Then Saul saw the ghost of Samuel rise before him, and bowed down with his face to the ground. The phantom asked him, "Why have you disquieted me, to bring me up?" and Saul answered, "I am sore distressed; for the Philistines make war against me, and God is departed from me, and answers me no more, neither by prophets nor by dreams; therefore I have called you up to tell me what I shall do." Then it said, "Why do you ask of me, seeing the Lord is departed from you and is become your enemy, and has rent the kingdom out of your hand? You and all Israel are delivered into the hand of the Philistines; and to-morrow you shall be with me." With these words it sank under earth again, and Saul fell down in a swoon; for he had eaten nothing for a day and a night, and had no strength left. At last the witch and his two servants roused him and laid him on a bed and prepared food for him; then they ate and rose up hastily and went away while it was still night.

CHAPTER CIX
THE WOEFUL BATTLE ON MOUNT GILBOA

THE next day the battle was fought on Mount Gilboa; the army of Israel fled before the Philistines, and there was a great slaughter. Saul's three sons were killed fighting beside him, and he himself was mortally wounded by an arrow. When he could go no further, he bade his armour-bearer draw his sword and thrust him through, that the enemy might not take him prisoner and torture him. But the armour-bearer was afraid, and would not; so Saul fell on his own sword and died; and when his armour-bearer saw that he was dead, he also fell on his own sword and died with him. The Philistines came to strip the slain after the battle and found the dead king among them; the gold crown and armlet had been stolen from the body; but they cut off his head and fastened it in the temple of Dagon, and took his armour and put it in the temple of Ashtaroth, and hung up his headless body on the city wall. But the men of the City of Dry Stones, whom Saul had saved from their enemies when he was made king, came at night and took his body down from the wall and carried it home, and there they buried it and made great lamentation.

CHAPTER CX
THE STOLEN CROWN

THE third day after the battle, a man came running to David in his castle in the wilderness, with his clothes all torn and earth upon his head, and fell to the ground before him, saying, "The people are fled from the battle, and many are fallen and dead, and Saul and Jonathan his son are dead also." Now this was the man who had stolen the crown and armlet from Saul's dead body as it upon the battle-field. David asked him how he knew. "I was by chance on Mount Gilboa," he said, "and there I saw the king leaning on his spear, and the horsemen and chariots of the enemy close after him. The king called to me, and when I came, told me to kill him, for he could not stand up or go any further. Being sure that he could not live after he was fallen, I killed him, and took the crown from his head and the armlet from his arm, and brought them to you; see, here they are, O king." But David answered him, "Your blood be on your own head if your story is true, for you have slain the Lord's anointed;" and ordered one of his guards to cut him down where he stood; so the liar died. But David made great mourning for Saul and for Jonathan.

CHAPTER CXI
THE CASTLE OF ZION

THEN the men of Judah made David king in Hebron; but Abner, Saul's chief captain, took Eshbaal the son of Saul across the river, and proclaimed him king in Mahanaim; and for two years they were both kings and their captains fought with one another. But the house of Saul grew weaker and weaker, and at last Abner quarrelled with his master and went to Hebron to make peace with David. Now Joab, David's chief captain, had a blood-feud with Abner because he had killed one of Joab's brothers in battle. Joab was away on a foray when Abner came to Hebron; but he came back soon after Abner was gone, and was very angry with David for letting him go in safety. Then he sent a messenger after Abner to bring him back; and when he came, not suspecting any treachery, Joab took him aside and stabbed him in the city gate. Not long after, two of Eshbaal's officers murdered him in his bed, and brought his head to David; but for all their reward, David hanged them both in Hebron. So David was king over all Israel; and he besieged the castle of Zion, which was so strong that the garrison set blind and lame men on the ramparts in mockery of him; for they thought it impossible that their castle should be taken. But David took it by storm and lived in it, and built a palace and a city there, which is the city of Jerusalem.

CHAPTER CXII
THE TRIUMPH OF THE ARK

WHEN David was established in his kingdom he went to the City of Woods to fetch the ark of God from the house where it had been since it came back on the cart from the Philistines, and brought it up to his city of Jerusalem with music and rejoicing, and the king went dancing before the ark. But Queen Michal looked through a window and saw King David leaping and dancing before the ark, and despised him in her heart; and when he came back to the palace, she could not hold her tongue, but upbraided him for not behaving like a king; so David put her away from being the queen, and she lived as a childless widow until the day of her death. Then David counselled to build a great temple for the ark; but a word of God came to him saying, "Because you have shed much blood in war and still have wars all about you, you may not build the house of God's rest; but your son who will be king after you shall have peace all his days, and rest from his enemies and a quiet throne; and he shall build

God's house." So David set masons to hew stones, and gathered store of gold and silver and iron and brass, and cedar-trees out of Lebanon, that his son might find everything ready for building; and meanwhile he fought against the Philistines and the people of Edom and Ammon and the Syrians beyond the river, and won victories and great renown.

CHAPTER CXIII
THE THIRTY KNIGHTS

KING David had thirty mighty men; the first was Adino the Tachmonite who sat in the seat, chief among the captains, and prince among the thirty; he lifted up his spear against eight hundred men, and slew them at one time. Next to him were Eleazer and Shammah; and these were the first three. These three chiefs of the thirty came to David in harvest time, when he was in a hold, and the garrison of the Philistines was in Bethlehem. David looked across the valley of Rephaim to the town of Bethlehem where he had been born, and longed, and said, "Oh, that one would give me drink of the water of the well of Bethlehem which is by the gate!" Then these three mighty men broke through the whole host of the Philistines, and drew water out of the well of Bethlehem by the gate, and brought it to David. But he would not drink it, and poured it out on the ground before God, saying, " Be it far from me, O Lord, that I should drink this ; is not this the blood of the men that went in jeopardy of their lives for me ? " therefore he would not drink it. After these three, Abishai the brother of Joab was chief ; he lifted up his spear against three hundred, and slew them. Also when the Sitter on the High Place, the son of the giant in Gath, being girded with a new sword, thought to have slain David, Abishai succoured David and slew the Philistine. Next to him was Benaiah, the captain of the Greek guards, who had done many acts : he slew two lion-like men of Moab ; he went down and slew a lion in a pit in the time of snow ; also he slew an Egyptian, a goodly man; and the Egyptian had a spear in his hand, but he went up to him with a staff, and plucked the spear out of the Egyptian's hand, and slew him with his own spear. After these were the other five-and-twenty knights, all mighty men : among whom were Sibbechai, who slew Saph, one of the sons of the giant, and Elhanan and Jonathan, who slew the other two sons of the giant, and Uriah the Hittite.

CHAPTER CXIV
THE SHOT FROM THE WALL

AT the time of year when kings go forth to battle, David sent out Joab and his thirty knights with an army, and they besieged the city of Rabbah; but David himself stayed at Jerusalem. He was walking in an evening on the roof of his cedar palace, when he looked down and saw a very beautiful woman washing herself at a fountain below. He sent to find out who she was, and they told him she was Bathsheba, the wife of Uriah the Hittite. David desired to have her for his own wife. He sent a message to the army for Uriah to come home, and tell him how the war was going. Then he kept him for two days feasting in the palace, and sent him back with a letter to carry to Joab, which said, "Set Uriah in the front of the battle where it is hottest, and retire from him, that he may be smitten and die." When Joab read the king's letter he ordered an attack on the city and set Uriah in front of the army. The men of the town sallied out, and the rest of the army fell back from Uriah, who was killed by a shot from the town wall; and a few more men who had stood by him were killed at the same time. Joab sent off a messenger to David immediately, and told him: "The king will be angry when he hears we have attacked the city and been beaten off, and will say, Why did you fight so near the city? Did you not know that they would shoot from the wall? who smote Abimelech the son of Gideon? did not a woman cast a piece of a millstone upon him from the wall, so that he died in Thisbe? Then say to him: Uriah the Hittite, your captain, is dead also." So the messenger took the news to David, who sent back word by him to Joab, saying, "Do not be troubled by this; for the sword devours one as well as another." Then as soon as Bathsheba had finished her mourning for Uriah, he had her brought to his palace, and married her, and they had a child.

CHAPTER CXV
THE STORY OF THE EWE-LAMB

THEN the prophet Nathan came to David and said, "O king, there were two men in one city, the one rich and the other poor. The rich man had many flocks and herds; the poor man had nothing but one little ewe-lamb, that lived with him and his children; it ate of his own meat and drank of his own cup, and lay in his bosom and was like a daughter to him. The rich man had to prepare food for a traveller who came to his house; and he grudged to take one of his own flocks and herds to dress and set before the traveller; but he took the poor man's lamb from him by violence and killed it and dressed it." David's anger was kindled, and he said, "By God's life, the man that did this deserves to be put to death; and he shall restore the lamb fourfold, because he did this thing and had no pity." Then Nathan answered David, "You are the man. The Lord God anointed you king over Israel, and delivered you out of the hand of Saul, and gave the people into your hand; and if that had been too little, he would have given you such and such things besides: why have you despised him, to do evil in his sight? You have killed Uriah the Hittite and taken his wife to be your wife; therefore the sword shall never depart from your house; God will raise up sorrow against you from your own family, and what was done secretly shall be punished before all Israel and before the sun.'

CHAPTER CXVI
THE SICK CHILD

THEN the child that had been born to David and Bathsheba fell ill; and David fasted and lay all night on the ground, and would not taste food or listen to his councillors. On the seventh day the child died. David's servants were afraid to tell him; but when he saw them whispering together, he asked, "Is the child dead?" and they said, "Yes." Then he rose and washed himself and ate bread. They asked him, "How is it that you fasted and wept for the child while it was alive, but rose and ate bread when it died?" and he answered them, "While the child was yet alive, I fasted and wept, for I said, Who can tell whether God will be pitiful to me, that the child may live? But now he is dead, why should I fast? can I bring him back again? I 'shall go to him, but he shall not return to me." So David took comfort, and went about the work of his kingdom; and afterwards David and Bathsheba had another child, whom they called Solomon.

CHAPTER CXVII
THE REBELLION OF ABSALOM

NO long time after, a bitter hatred broke out between David's eldest son Amnon and his second son Absalom, till, from bad to worse, Absalom killed his brother by treachery at a feast, and fled to the court of his grandfather, the king of the Passage of the Wilderness. After three years Absalom was allowed to come back, but for two years more he was shut up in his own house and David refused to see him. Then at last they were reconciled, and Absalom became heir to the kingdom; but he was not content with this, and conspired to dethrone his father David and make himself king. Absalom was the most beautiful man in all Israel, and lived in great state, with fifty men that ran before him wherever he went; and he was gracious to all, and when he heard of any man that lacked justice he would say, "O that I were judge in the land, that every man that had a suit or cause might come to me, and I would do him justice!" So he stole the people's hearts away; and at last he proclaimed himself king at Hebron with sound of trumpet, and the people gathered round him. Ahithophel, the wisest of David's councillors, joined him there, and ruled everything by his counsel. When news came to David that the whole nation went after Absalom, and that he was preparing to march on Jerusalem, he left his palace of Zion and fled into the wilderness. All his household went on in front, except a few women who were left to keep the house; then the king followed with his Greek guards and his captains (for they remained faithful to him), and they all crossed the valley and went up the ascent of Mount Olivet, barefoot and with covered heads, weeping as they went.

CHAPTER CXVIII
THE FLIGHT INTO THE WILDERNESS

AT the top of the hill, Hushai of Erech, one of David's councillors, came to join him, with his coat rent and earth upon his head. David said to him, "If you come with me, you will be of no use to me; return to the city and join Absalom and pretend to be his servant, and so you may help me by thwarting the counsel of Ahithophel." So Hushai returned, and as he came into the city by one gate, Absalom and his men came in by another. By this time David was beyond the top of the hill; and there Shimei the son of Gera, a man of the house of Saul, came out on the hillside as he passed, and threw stones at him and cursed, crying, "Come out, come out, you bloody man." Then Abishai, David's nephew, said to him, "Why should this dead dog curse my lord the king? Let me go over, I pray you, and take off his head." But David said, "Let him curse; behold, my son seeks my life; how much more may this Benjamite do it? Let him alone, and it may be that God will requite me good for his cursing this day."

CHAPTER CXIX
THE COUNSEL OF AHITHOPHEL

MEANWHILE Absalom was holding a council in the palace; and Ahithophel advised, "Let me pursue David this same evening with a small force, and come on him suddenly at night while he is weary and weak-handed; then all the people who are with him will take to flight, and we shall seize David alone and kill him, and the war will be over; and I will bring back all the people to you, as a bride is brought to her husband." This advice pleased the council well. Then Absalom said, "Call Hushai also, and let us hear what he says." So Hushai was brought in, and Absalom said to him, "Ahithophel has spoken after this manner; shall we do accordingly? If not, speak." Then Hushai said, "Ahithophel's counsel is not wise. Your father is a good captain, and his guards are mighty men; you will not take them by surprise; if you pursue him hastily he will lie in ambush in a valley and attack you unawares, and if some of your men fall, the cry will go abroad that there is a slaughter among the people that follow

Absalom, and the hearts of the people will melt. My counsel therefore is this: Gather all Israel together and go forth yourself at the head of a great army; then wherever we find David we shall surround him and swallow him up; or if he have taken shelter in a city, we shall bring ropes and draw the city into the river, until there be not one small stone left where it stood."

CHAPTER CXX
THE WELL IN THE COURTYARD

HUSHAI'S advice pleased Absalom more than Ahithophel's; and so it was determined, and the council broke up. Now David had left two of his men by a fountain outside the city (for they dared not shew themselves in the city) to bring him news. Hushai sent a girl out to tell them what had been determined at the council, and to warn David not to stop the night in the plain. But a boy saw them hiding by the fountain, and told Absalom, who sent soldiers after them; then they crept down into a well in the court of a house, and the woman of the house put a lid on the well's mouth and spread a heap of corn over it. When Absalom's men came and asked where they were, she said, "They have gone over the brook of water." So they searched, but could not find them, and returned into the city. Then the men climbed out of the well and ran to tell David; so he went on all through the night, and by the next day's dawn had crossed Jordan and was safe in the wilderness. But Ahithophel, when he saw that his counsel was not followed, saddled his ass and rode home to his own city, and hanged himself in his house.

CHAPTER CXXI
THE BATTLE IN THE WOOD

DAVID gathered an army in the wilderness, and there was a great battle in the wood of Ephraim. Absalom fought at the head of his men, but David could not bear to go out to battle; he watched his army march through the city-gate, and gave charge to his captains in the hearing of all the army to deal gently with Absalom. When the armies met, Absalom's men fled and there was a great slaughter in the wood. As Absalom rode under a great oak in the forest, a low bough caught his head; his long hair, of which he was so proud that he only had it cut once a year, was entangled in the branches, and his mule went away from under him, so that he was left hanging in the oak-tree between heaven and earth. One of David's soldiers saw this happen, and ran to tell Joab. "Why did you not strike him to the ground?" said Joab, "and I would have given you ten pieces of silver." "I would not touch him for a thousand pieces of silver," he answered; "nothing is long hid from our lord the king, and you would have been the first to put me to death for disobeying his orders." "I cannot waste time talking," Joab said; and with that he galloped up to the oak and ran Absalom through the body with his spear. Then he blew a trumpet to stop the pursuit, and they took Absalom's body and flung it into a pit in the wood, and threw a great heap of stones over it; and his army fled and dispersed, each man to his own home.

CHAPTER CXXII
THE TWO RUNNERS

FORTHWITH two runners started to run to the city and take the king news of the battle. David was sitting in the gateway between the inner and outer gate, and a watchman stood on the roof of the gateway-tower and looked across the plain. The watchman saw a single man come running in the distance, and cried to the king; who said, "If he be alone, there is tidings in his mouth;" and the runner came apace and drew near. Then the watchman espied another man running, and called down to the gate; and the king said, "He also brings tidings." Presently the watchman said, "Methinks the running of the foremost is like the running of Ahimaaz son of Zadok." "He is a good man, and comes with good tidings," said the king. Then Ahimaaz came up running, and cried to the king, "Peace!" and fell down on his face before him, and said, "Blessed be the Lord, who has put down those who rose up against my lord the king." But David only said, "Is the young man Absalom safe?" Ahimaaz answered, "When I was sent, I saw a great tumult, but I do not know what it was about." "Turn aside, and stand there," said the king. In a few minutes more the second runner, who was David's negro servant, came up, and cried, "Tidings, my lord the king: for the Lord has avenged you this day of all that rose up against you." But the king said, "Is the young man Absalom safe?" He answered, "May the enemies of my lord the king, and all that rise against you to do you hurt, be as that young man is." And the king was much moved, and went up to the chamber over the gate, weeping; and as he went, he said, "O my son Absalom, my son, my son Absalom, would God I had died for you, O Absalom, my son, my son!"

CHAPTER CXXIII
THE SORROWFUL VICTORY

SO the victory that day was turned into mourning, when word went among the people how the king was grieved for his son, and they crept by stealth into the city, as shamed men steal away when they have fled in battle. At last Joab went in to the king, and told him that he had shamed the faces of all his servants, who had fought for him and saved his life: "For I see," he said, "that if Absalom had lived and all we had died, it would have pleased you well. Now rise and go forth, or I swear by God it will be worse for you than all the evil that has befallen you from your youth up till now." Then the king rose, and sat in the gate. But he never forgave Joab: and when he was dying, he charged his son Solomon, who became king after him, to put Joab to death as a traitor and murderer.

CHAPTER CXXIV
THE CITY OF MEADOWS

THUS the war ended; but when David returned from the wilderness to his kingdom, the men of Judah began to quarrel with the men of Israel over their shares in bringing him back; and the quarrel grew so fierce that when a man of Benjamin called Sheba blew a trumpet and cried, "We have no part in David," the tribes followed him and revolted from David; only the army and the men of Judah remained loyal to him. Joab went out with the army and besieged

Sheba in the City of Meadows, and filled up the moat with a mound and began to batter the wall. Then a wise woman out of the city cried to Joab to come near and speak with her. When he came, she said, "You seek to destroy a city and a mother in Israel; why will you swallow up the inheritance of the Lord?" He answered, "Far be it from me to swallow up or destroy; but a man of Mount Ephraim, Sheba by name, has rebelled against the king; give him up to me, and I will take away my army from your city." She said, "His head shall be thrown to you over the wall." Then the woman went to all the people in her wisdom, and they cut off Sheba's head and threw it out to Joab. So he blew the trumpet to retire, and all the people dispersed to their homes, and the revolt came to an end.

CHAPTER CXXV
THE WATCHING OF RIZPAH

THERE was a famine in the days of David for three years, year after year, and when he enquired of the precious stones, they answered, "It is for Saul and his bloody house, because he slew the Gibeonites." For Joshua and the children of Israel had sworn safety to the Gibeonites when they conquered the land; but Saul had sought to destroy them, and broken the oath. David said to the Gibeonites, "What shall I do for you? wherewith shall I make atonement, that you may bless the inheritance of the Lord?" They answered, "We will have no silver nor gold in repayment; but let seven of the sons of the man who destroyed us be delivered to us, that we may hang them on the hill." Then the king took the two sons of Rizpah the daughter of Aiah, whom she bore to Saul, and the five sons of Merab the daughter of Saul, and delivered them to the Gibeonites; and they hanged them on the hill under the open sky, all seven together, at the beginning of harvest time. But Rizpah the daughter of Aiah took sackcloth and spread it upon the rock, and kept the birds of the air off them by day and the beasts of the field by night, sitting there night and day from the beginning of harvest all through the burning summer till the winter rains dropped on them out of heaven. When this was told the king, he took their bones and buried them all together in the burying-place of their family; and after that the land had peace.

CHAPTER CXXVI
THE ANGEL'S SWORD

DAVID offended God in numbering the people; and the prophet Gad came to him, saying, "Choose one of three things: Shall seven years of famine come unto you in your land? or will you flee three months before your enemies while they pursue you? or shall there be three days' pestilence in your land? Now advise, and see what answer I shall return to him that sent me." David chose the last, "For the Lord's mercies are many," he said; "let us fall into his hand and not into the hand of man." So at morning the Angel of the Pestilence went forth among the people, and between morning and midday had destroyed seventy thousand men. At noon he reached Jerusalem and stood over the city by the threshing-floor of Araunah; and when David looked up, he saw the angel stand between earth and heaven, with a drawn sword in his hand stretched out over Jerusalem. Then David and all the elders of Israel fell upon their faces in prayer; and God was appeased, and said to the angel, "It is enough; stay your hand,"

and the angel put up his sword into the sheath. Then David would have bought the threshing-floor from Araunah to build an altar on it; but Araunah gave him the floor and the oxen without payment, as a king to a king. So David built an altar there and offered sacrifice, and God answered him by fire upon the altar out of heaven.

CHAPTER CXXVII
THE CHOICE IN THE DREAM

WHEN David grew old and near his death he had his son Solomon crowned to be king after him; Solomon rode down the city on the royal mule with the Greek guards round him, and they blew the silver trumpets and set the crown on his head and proclaimed him king, and the whole people made rejoicing. So David died, and Solomon was king. Then God appeared to Solomon in a dream by night and told him to ask a gift; and in his dream Solomon said, "O Lord, thou hast made me king instead of David my father, and I am like a little child who does not know how to go out or come in: give me therefore wisdom to judge thy people, and to discern between good and bad." God answered him: "Because you have asked this thing, and have not asked long life, nor riches, nor victory, see, I have given you a wise heart such as no man has had before, nor shall any man have after; and also I have given you besides that which you have not asked for, riches, and honour, and length of days." So Solomon awoke out of his dream.

CHAPTER CXXVIII
THE JUDGMENT OF SOLOMON

IN the morning two women came before Solomon as he sat upon his throne, and cried to him for judgment. Each of them was carrying a baby, but one of the two babies was dead. The one woman cried to the king and said: "O my lord, I and this woman live in one house together alone, with no one else in the house, and we each of us bore a child, the one within three days of the other. But last night this woman's child died in the night, because she overlaid it; and she rose in the middle of the night and took my baby from me while I slept, and laid her own dead baby in my bosom; but when I saw it by daylight, it was not my child, the son that I bore." Then the other woman said, "No; but the living child is mine, and the dead is yours;" and the first cried again, "No; but the dead is yours, and the living is mine." Thus they spoke before the king; and there was no one to bear witness to one or the other. The king said, "Bring me a sword." When it was brought, he said, "Divide the living child in two, and give half to the one woman, and half to the other." But the woman who had spoken first, and whose child it really was, cried out to the king, "O my lord, give her the child, and slay it not!" for her heart melted over her child. King Solomon answered and said, "Give her the living child; she is its mother." All the people heard of this judgment of Solomon and praised it, and saw that the wisdom of God was in him to do justice.

CHAPTER CXXIX
THE GLORY OF SOLOMON

IN king Solomon's days the people were as the sand by the sea in multitude, eating and drinking and making merry. He reigned over all the kings round about him, and had peace all his days; the people lived safely under him, every man under his vine and under his fig-tree. He had four thousand chariots and forty thousand chariot-horses; he made silver and gold as plentiful as stones, and cedar trees as common wood. He built Tadmor in the wilderness, and many other great cities with walls and brazen bars. All the dishes in his palace, and in the House of the Forest of Lebanon which he built, were of pure gold. He had ships in his harbours that sailed to Tarshish and the furthest southern seas; the voyage took three years to go and return, and once in every three years his fleet came back bringing gold and silver and ivory, and apes and peacocks; and he built another fleet on the Arabian gulf, that sailed to Ophir and brought back gold and sandalwood and precious stones. So he was richer than all other kings; also God gave him such wisdom as excelled all the wisdom of the children of the East, and all the wisdom of Egypt. He made three thousand proverbs, and a thousand and five songs; and he had all knowledge of trees, from the cedar of Lebanon to the weed that grows out of the wall, and of beasts and birds and fishes and insects; so that the kings of the peoples of the earth came out of all lands to hear his wisdom.

CHAPTER CXXX
THE BUILDING OF THE TEMPLE

THE greatest of all Solomon's works was the temple that he built at Jerusalem, of hewn stone and cedarwood, with a pillared porch before it carved over with lilies, and windows of narrow lights along either wall. The stone of which it was built was quarried underground and made ready before it was brought up, so that the house rose silently, and no noise of hammer or axe or any tool of iron was heard in it while it was building. The roof was of cedar beams brought by sea on rafts from the forests of Lebanon, and the floor and the panelling of the walls were of cedar, and the whole of the house within was carved with cherubim and palm-trees and lions and wild vines and open flowers, and all the carving overlaid with pure gold. In the temple was an inner chamber, called the Holy of Holies, shut off by golden lattice work and a curtain of blue and purple and crimson with cherubim wrought into it. In the Holy of Holies stood two great golden cherubim each sixteen feet high, with vast outstretched wings; their wings reached across the chamber outwards to either wall and inwards till they touched one another in the middle of the house; and when the temple was finished, the ark of God was set in the Holy of Holies under the wings of the covering cherubim, and the curtain drawn before it, and it remained there in thick darkness except when the glory of God descended upon it and lighted up all the golden room.

CHAPTER CXXXI
THE FEAST OF THE DEDICATION

IN front of the temple stood two great pillars of brass seventy feet high, one on each side of the doorway, with a raised pattern on them of lilies and pomegranates; and all round the inner court ran a triple cloister of stone, roofed with cedar. In this inner court stood Solomon's molten sea, which he had cast of brass and adorned round the edge with lilies and wild vines cast in the metal; it rested on the backs of twelve oxen of brass that stood in a circle under it, all looking outwards; and it held water for two thousand baths. But in the temple itself all the metal work, even the nails and the door-hinges, was of pure gold. At the dedication of the temple, King Solomon made a feast to all the people for seven days; all the priests and singers of the whole land were assembled together, dressed in white linen, with cymbals and harps and psalteries, and with them a hundred and twenty priests to sound upon trumpets; and at a signal all the trumpeters sounded together and the singers lifted up their voice as one man with the trumpets and cymbals, and sang, "PRAISE THE LORD, FOR HE IS GOOD; FOR HIS MERCY ENDURETH FOR EVER." Then a bright cloud filled the temple, so that the priests could not stand to minister; for the glory of God had filled his house.

CHAPTER CXXXII
THE CEDAR PALACE

SOLOMON also built the palace of the Forest of Lebanon, which was panelled with cedar and ivory, and stood on four rows of cedar pillars, with a cedar portico in front of it, and two inner courts built of costly stones, one for himself and the other for the queen his wife, who was the daughter of king Pharaoh of Egypt.

When the palace was finished, the queen was brought into it with great rejoicing, carried on cushions of tapestry and dressed all in cloth of gold, with spices burning round her and music sounding out of the ivory palace to welcome her in. In the portico of the palace was King Solomon's throne of judgment from which he judged the people, of ivory and gold; six steps went up to it, and upon each step stood two golden lions, one on either side, twelve lions in all; there was not the like of it in any kingdom.

CHAPTER CXXXIII
THE QUEEN OF SHEBA

THE Queen of Sheba heard of the fame of Solomon, and of his riches and wisdom, and came from very far to visit him, with a great train of camels bearing spices and gold and precious stones. She proved Solomon with hard questions, and he answered them all; and when she heard his wisdom, and saw the splendour of his house, and the dresses of his servants and his cupbearers, and the bridge by which he went up to the house of God, she fell into a swoon; and when she came to herself she gave Solomon great gifts of gold and spice and precious stones (no such spices were ever brought to the land again), and returned into the south to her own land.

CHAPTER CXXXIV
THE DIVISION OF THE KINGDOMS

BUT the labour that built the temple and the palace, and the wealth that was spent on the splendours of Solomon's court, was all wrung out of the people; and though they were proud of Solomon's glory, the burdens that he laid on them were very heavy to bear; so that when he died and his son Rehoboam became king after him, all the people assembled under Jeroboam the son of Nebat, and asked the new king to make their burdens lighter than they had been in the days of Solomon. Rehoboam told them to come back for their answer in three days, and meanwhile he called his council. The old men who had been Solomon's councillors advised him to give a fair answer to the people. "Be their servant to-day," they said, "and you will have them for your servants for ever." But the young men of his own age, who had grown up with him, advised him to answer the people roughly, and say, "My little finger shall be thicker than my father's loins; my father chastised you with whips, but I will chastise you with scorpions." On the third day Jeroboam and all the people came for their answer, and the king answered them according to the counsel of the young men, saying, "My father made your burden heavy, but I will add to it; he chastised you with whips, but I will chastise you with scorpions." When the people heard this they cried out, "To your tents, O Israel: now see to your own house, David!" and all the tribes except Judah revolted from king Rehoboam and made Jeroboam king over Israel. So the kingdom was divided, and from that day forth there were two kingdoms, one of Judah and one of Israel. But Jeroboam feared that if his people went up to Jerusalem to sacrifice at Solomon's temple, their heart might turn again to the house of David; therefore he made two golden calves and set them up in two of his cities, Bethel and Dan, and said, "It is too much for you to go up to Jerusalem to worship; behold your gods, O Israel, which brought you out of the land of Egypt."

CHAPTER CXXXV
THE MAN OF GOD FROM JUDAH

A MAN of God out of Judah came to Bethel while king Jeroboam stood by the altar burning incense before his golden calf, and cried against the altar, saying, "O altar, altar, a child shall be born to the house of David, who shall offer on you the priests of the high places that burn incense on you, and men's bones shall be burnt upon you." The king stretched out his hand, crying, "Lay hold on him!" when at once his hand stiffened so that he could not draw it back again; and the altar was rent asunder and the ashes poured out of it. But the man of God returned to go home by another way; for God had said, when he sent him, "Eat no bread, nor drink water there, nor turn again by the same way that you came." Now there was an old prophet in Bethel, whose sons came and told him of the man out of Judah, and what he had done that day. He told them to saddle his ass, and mounted and rode after the man of God till he found him sitting by the wayside under an oak. He asked him, "Are you the man of God that came from Judah?" and he answered, "I am." Then he said, "Come home with me and eat bread." But the man of God answered, "I may not; for the word of the Lord said to me, Eat no bread nor drink water there, nor turn again to go by the way that you came." The old prophet said, "I am a prophet also as you are; and an angel spoke a word of the Lord to me also, saying, Bring him back with you to your house, that he may eat bread and drink water." But he lied. So the man of God went back with him. But while they sat at table, the word of the Lord came indeed to the old prophet, and he cried to the man of God and said, "Because you have disobeyed the mouth of the Lord, and have eaten bread and drunk water in the place of which the Lord said to you, Eat no bread, nor drink water there, your body shall never be laid in the grave of your fathers." After they had eaten and drunk, the man of God saddled his ass and went on his way; and on his way a lion met him and killed him. His dead body lay in the road with his ass standing by it, and the lion stood over it all day. Men passed by and saw this sight and brought the news to the city. When the old prophet heard of it, he rode forth and found him lying so with his ass beside him and the lion standing by; but the lion had not touched the body, nor hurt the ass. The old prophet took up the dead man and laid him on his ass and brought him back to the city, and there buried him in his own grave; and they mourned over him, saying, "Alas, my brother!" Then he said to his sons, "When I am dead, bury me in the grave where the man of God is buried; lay my bones beside his bones; for the saying which he cried against the altar and against the high places shall surely come."

CHAPTER CXXXVI
THE WIDOW'S JAR

AHAB son of Omri reigned over Israel, and married Jezebel, the princess of Sidon. He set up altars to Baal and Asherah, the gods of Sidon, and served them; therefore God sent word to him by the prophet Elijah of Thisbe, that there were to be three years of drought and famine in the land. When Elijah had given his message to the king, he went away and lived in hiding by a brook in the desert; he drank the water of the brook, and every day, morning and evening, ravens brought him bread and meat. After a while the brook dried up because there was no rain, and he had to leave that place. He went to a town, and outside the town gate he found a widow woman gathering sticks, and asked her to give him a morsel of bread. She said, "I have no food left but a handful of meal in a barrel and a little oil in a jar; I am gathering two sticks to light a fire and bake a cake for myself and my son, that we may eat our last meal and die." Elijah answered, "Go and do so; but make me a cake first, and the barrel of meal shall not waste, nor the jar of oil fail, until the day that God gives rain upon the earth." So she went and did as he said; and for a full year she and her house lived upon the barrel of meal that wasted not and the jar of oil that did not fail.

CHAPTER CXXXVII
THE ALTARS ON MOUNT CARMEL

IN the third year of the famine, the word of God came to Elijah, saying, "Go, show yourself to Ahab, and I will send rain." So he went to the king, and said to him, "Send, and gather all Israel upon Mount Carmel, and let the four hundred and fifty prophets of Baal and the four hundred prophets of Asherah be there, who eat at the queen's table." The people gathered on Carmel; and Elijah said to them, "I only remain a prophet of the Lord, but Baal's prophets are four hundred and fifty men; let us then build two altars, and lay sacrifices on them, but kindle no fire; then let them call on the name of Baal, and I will call on the name of the Lord; and let the God be God that answers by fire." All the people said, "It is well spoken." So the priests of Baal made their altar and called on their god from morning till noon, crying, "O Baal, hear us!" but there was no voice, nor any that answered. At noon Elijah mocked them, and said, "Cry aloud, for he is a god; either he is talking, or he is pursuing, or he is on a journey, or perhaps he sleeps, and must be awaked." So they cried aloud and cut themselves with knives after their manner from midday till the time of evening prayer; but there was no voice nor answer, nor any that regarded. Then Elijah built his altar of twelve great stones, and made a trench round about it; he laid his sacrifice on the altar, and had twelve barrels of water brought from the river and poured over the altar until it filled the trench. Then Elijah cried to God, and the fire of the Lord fell and consumed the sacrifice and the stones of the altar and licked up the water in the trench; and when the people saw it they fell on their faces, and cried, "The Lord is God, the Lord is God!"

CHAPTER CXXXVIII
THE LITTLE CLOUD

THEN Elijah said to Ahab, "Arise, eat and drink; for there is a sound of a noise of rain." So Ahab arose to eat and drink; but Elijah went up to the top of Carmel and threw himself down on the ground with his face between his knees and said to his servant, "Climb up, and look toward the sea." He climbed up and looked, and said, "I see nothing." Elijah bade him look again, but still he saw nothing; and so he looked seven times, and at the seventh time he said, "I see a little cloud rising out of the sea like a man's hand." Then Elijah said, "Go, say to Ahab, Yoke and get you down, that the rain stop you not." In a little while the heaven was black with clouds and wind, and there was a great rain, so that the floods came out and covered the roads behind Ahab as he drove back across the plain to his palace.

CHAPTER CXXXIX
THE STILL SMALL VOICE

WHEN Queen Jezebel heard of what Elijah had done on Carmel she threatened to kill him; so he fled out of the land and went a day's journey into the wilderness. There he lay down under a bush of broom and prayed that he might die, saying, "It is enough; now, O Lord, take away my life, for I am not better than my fathers." Then he fell asleep there under the bush of broom, until an angel touched him and said, "Rise and eat." He awoke and looked, and saw a cake baked among the embers and a jug of water standing at his head; so he ate and drank, and went in the strength of that meat forty days and forty nights, to the mount of God in the wilderness. He lodged in a cave on the mountain; and the voice of God came to him there, saying, "What are you doing here, Elijah?" He answered, "The children of Israel have forsaken thee, thrown down thine altars and slain thy prophets; I only am left; and they seek my life to take it away." The voice said, "Go forth and stand upon the mount before the Lord." Elijah waited for the Lord to pass by: and first a great wind rent the mountains and broke the rocks in pieces before him; but the Lord was not in the wind: and after the wind an earthquake; but the Lord was not in the earthquake: and after the earthquake a fire; but the Lord was not in the fire: and after the fire a still small voice. Elijah wrapped his face in his mantle and went out, and stood in the entrance of the cave. There the voice came to him and said again, "What are you doing here, Elijah?" and he answered as before. Then the voice of the Lord said, "Go, return; I have yet left seven thousand in Israel whose knees have not bowed to Baal and whose mouth has not kissed him." So Elijah went back to find king Ahab.

CHAPTER CXL
NABOTH'S VINEYARD

ALONGSIDE of the palace of king Ahab in Jezreel there was a vineyard belonging to Naboth the Jezreelite. The king wished to have it to make it into a garden for himself, and offered to buy it of Naboth or give him a better vineyard in exchange for it. But Naboth would not part with it, because it had belonged to his family for a long while; and the king was so displeased that he lay down on his bed with his face turned away to the wall, and would not eat. Queen Jezebel came and asked what ailed him; and when he told her, she said to him, "Are you not king of Israel? Rise and eat and be merry, for I will give you Naboth's vineyard." Then she wrote letters to the nobles of the city, sealed with the royal seal, ordering them to seize Naboth and hire false witness against him, and so put him to death. They obeyed the queen; Naboth was seized and dragged before a meeting of the people, and two men swore falsely that they had heard him curse his lord the king; then they carried him out of the city, and stoned him and his children to death, and sent word to the queen. She went in to king Ahab and said, " Naboth is dead, and has left no children; go, take possession of his vineyard." So Ahab went down to the vineyard; and there in the vineyard Elijah was waiting for him. " Have you found me, O mine enemy?" said the king. Elijah answered, " Have you killed, and also taken possession? Thus saith the Lord, In the place where dogs licked the blood of Naboth shall dogs lick your blood; God will bring evil on you and cut off your household, and dogs shall eat Jezebel by the city ditch."

CHAPTER CXLI
THE COUNCIL OF THE KINGS

JEHOSHAPHAT king of Judah made alliance with king Ahab, and came to visit him in the ivory house that he had built for himself at Samaria; and there the two kings planned a war against the Syrians, sitting in their striped robes on two thrones by the city gate. Jehoshaphat said, " Let us enquire at the mouth of the Lord, whether we shall go against Ramoth-Gilead to battle." Ahab called all his four hundred prophets; and they said with one voice, "Go, for God shall deliver it into the king's hand." Then Jehoshaphat asked, "Is there not a prophet of the Lord besides, of whom we may enquire?" Ahab answered, "There is one, Micaiah the son of Imlah; but I hate him; for he never prophesies good of me, but always evil." However, he was sent for; and the messenger who fetched him said to him, "All the prophets are prophesying good with one mouth; you had much better do the same." But he said, "By God's life, what the Lord says to me, that will I speak;" so he came before the two kings, and Ahab asked him, "Micaiah, shall we go against Ramoth-Gilead to battle?" He answered, "I saw the Lord sitting on his throne, and all the host of heaven standing by him on right and left, and the Lord said, Who shall entice Ahab, that he may go and fall at Ramoth-Gilead? One said this, and another that; then a spirit came forth and stood before the Lord and said, I will entice him. The Lord said to Him, How? and he said, I will go forth and be a lying spirit in the mouth of all his prophets. And God said, You shall entice, and prevail; go forth." Ahab said to Jehoshaphat, "Did I not tell you that he would prophesy no good of me?" Then he said to his guards, "Take this fellow away, and keep him in prison on bread and water till I return in peace." But Micaiah said, "If you return in peace at all, the Lord has not spoken by me." So the two kings went to Ramoth-Gilead.

CHAPTER CXLII
THE RANDOM ARROW

THERE the two kings joined battle with the Syrians; and the king of Judah went into battle in his royal robes, but Ahab disguised himself as a common soldier that he might not be known; for the king of Syria had ordered his captains to fight only against Ahab. But when the battle began a certain man drew a bow at aventure, and the arrow struck Ahab between the joints of his armour. All day the battle went on, and king Ahab held himself up in his chariot till evening, slowly bleeding to death. About sunset, word ran through the army of Israel that the king was dead, and they broke and fled, each to his own city. But the dead king was brought back in his chariot to Samaria, where they buried him; and the chariot and armour were washed in the pool outside the city, and there the dogs licked up his blood.

CHAPTER CXLIII
THE CHARIOT OF FIRE

ELIJAH and his servant Elisha went together through the land; and as they went, the prophets came out of the towns to meet them, and said to Elisha, "Do you know that the Lord will take away your master from you to-day?" He said, "Yes, I know." So they passed on, and came to the river Jordan, and fifty of the prophets stood watching them by the river bank. Then Elijah took off his mantle and struck the water with it, and the river was divided, so that they went over on dry ground. When they had crossed the river, they went on, talking as they went; and suddenly a chariot of fire with horses of fire appeared and parted them asunder, and Elijah went up in the chariot of fire by a whirlwind into heaven. Elisha looked up till he could see him no longer; then he took

Elijah's mantle, which had fallen from him as he went up to heaven, and went back and stood by the bank of Jordan, and struck the water with it, saying, "Where is the Lord God of Elijah?" The water divided and let him cross over; and the prophets who were watching came to meet him and bowed down before him.

CHAPTER CXLIV
THE LADY OF SHUNEM

ELISHA passed through Shunem, where there was a great lady, and she made him eat bread at her house; and afterwards as often as he passed by, he turned in there. Then she said to her husband, "This is a holy man; let us make a little chamber on the wall, and furnish it for him with a bed and a table and a stool and a candlestick, that he may lie there whenever he comes to us." Elisha wished to make her some return for her kindness; and first he asked her, "Shall I speak for you to the king?" But she said, "I am content to live here among my own people." Then he found that the one thing she desired was a child, for she had none; so he called her and said,

"Within a year you shall hold a son in your arms." The next year she bore a son. When her child was big enough to walk alone, he went out one day in harvest time among the reapers. The heat of the sun made him ill, and he cried to his father, "My head, my head." A lad carried him back to the house to his mother; and he sat on her lap in the house till noon, and then died. She took her dead child up and laid him on Elisha's bed, and went out, shutting the door behind her; then she told a servant to saddle an ass, and rode across the plain through the heat of the day without slacking, till she came to Elisha's house on Mount Carmel; and there she fell at his feet, crying, "Did I ask a son of you, my lord?" Elisha rose and rode back with her, and went up to the little room on the wall where the dead child was lying on his bed. He went in and shut the door and prayed to God, and then bowed himself over the child, putting his mouth upon his mouth, and his eyes upon his eyes, and his hands upon his hands; and the child grew warm, and sneezed seven times, and opened his eyes. Then Elisha called the mother, who came and fell at his feet and took her child alive and well from his hands.

CHAPTER CXLV
THE SYRIAN CAPTAIN

NAAMAN, captain of the host of the king of Syria, was a great man and a valiant, but he was a leper. In his house was a little maid out of the land of Israel, who had been taken captive by a band of Syrians, and waited on Naaman's wife. She said to her mistress, "Would God that my lord were with the prophet in Samaria; for he would recover him of his leprosy." The king of Syria heard of this, and said to Naaman, "At least go and try what the prophet in Samaria can do for you; I will give you a letter to his master the king of Israel." So Naaman went with a great train of servants and mules laden with gold and silver, and delivered his master's letter to the king of Israel. The king read the letter till he came to the place where it said, "And now with this letter I have sent my servant Naaman to you, that you may recover him of his leprosy;" then he tore his robes for spite, and said to his court, "Am I God, to kill and make alive, that this man sends to me to cure a man of leprosy? See how he seeks a quarrel against me." But Elisha sent word to the king, "Send the Syrian to me, and he shall know that there is a prophet in Israel." So Naaman came in his chariot to Elisha's door; and Elisha sent out a message to him, "Go and wash seven times in Jordan, and you shall be cured." At this Naaman fell into a rage: "Why did he not come out himself," he said, "and strike me with his mantle to cure me? and why does he bid me go and wash in Jordan? are not my own rivers at Damascus better than all the rivers in Israel?" and he turned to go away in his anger. But his servants came about him and pacified him. "O our lord," they said, "if he had told you to do some hard thing, would you not have done it? and this is an easy thing that he tells you to do." So Naaman went and dipped seven times in Jordan, and at once became well.

CHAPTER CXLVI

THE BAGS OF SILVER

NAAMAN came back to thank Elisha, and ask him to accept a present; but he would not take anything; so Naaman went away to go home. Then Elisha's servant Gehazi thought to himself, "My master has spared this Syrian; but by God's life, I will run after him and get something from him." So when Naaman had got a little way he ran after the chariot, and Naaman, when he saw him come running, stopped and alighted, and asked, "Is all well?" He said, "All is well; but two young prophets have just come to visit my master, and he has sent me to ask you for a bag of silver and some clothes for them." Naaman answered, "By all means; but take two bags of silver, one for each of them;" and he sent two of his men back with Gehazi, carrying the silver and the clothes. When they got to the house, he put the silver in the turret-room, and the men went back to their master; then he went in and waited on Elisha. Presently Elisha asked him, "Where have you been, Gehazi?" He answered, "Your servant has been nowhere." But Elisha said, "Went not my heart with you, when the man turned from his chariot? Is this a time to take money, and buy vineyards and oliveyards and sheep and oxen and servants? The leprosy of Naaman therefore shall be upon you for ever." And he went out from his master's presence a leper as white as snow.

CHAPTER CXLVII
THE BLIND ARMY

THE king of Syria made war against the king of Israel; but when he planned an attack on any place, Elisha sent word to the king of Israel, who put a garrison there. This happened more than once or twice, so that the king of Syria thought there must be a traitor in his household, till one of his servants said, "The prophet in Israel tells his master the very words that you speak in your bedchamber." Then he sent men with horses and chariots to take Elisha prisoner. Elisha lived then in a town on the top of a hill; and they came by night, and surrounded the hill on every side. Early in the morning Elisha's servant went out, and seeing the valley full of Syrians, ran back to his master, crying, "Alas, what will become of us?" But he answered, "Fear not; there are more with us than with them; Lord, open his eyes, that he may see." Then the young man's eyes were opened, and he saw the whole hillside between the town and the Syrians full of chariots and horses of fire. But God smote the Syrians with blindness, so that they did not know where they were; and Elisha went down and said to them, "This is not the way; follow me, and I will lead you to the man whom you seek." So they followed him, and he led them into Samaria; then their eyes were opened again, and they found themselves in the middle of Samaria, with the king of Israel's army all round about them. The king asked Elisha, "Shall I kill them?" but he answered, "Would you kill those whom you had taken captive with your sword and bow? let them eat and drink and go back to their master." So for a while the Syrians ceased to trouble the land of Israel.

CHAPTER CXLVIII
THE FAMINE IN SAMARIA

AFTERWARDS war broke out again, and the king of Syria laid siege to Samaria. There was a great famine in the city, but Elisha shut himself up in his house and did nothing. When the famine was at its worst, a woman came and cried to the king of Israel, Joram son of Ahab, as he went along on the wall, "Help me, my lord, O king!" He said to her, "God's curse, how can I help you? out of the barn-floor, or out of the winepress? what ails you?" She answered, "My lord, this other woman said to me yesterday, Give your child, that we may eat him to-day, and we will eat my child to-morrow; so we boiled my child and ate him, and now to-day she has hidden her child and will not give him to be eaten." When the king heard this story, he rent his royal robe, so that people saw the sackcloth that he wore under it next his skin, and said, "God do so to me if the head of Elisha shall stand on his shoulders a day longer." But Elisha sat in his house; and when he heard steps outside, he said to the people that were with him, "See, this son of a murderer has sent to take away my head; shut the door and hold the messenger fast, for I hear the sound of his master's feet behind him." The words were hardly out of his mouth when the king himself came; then Elisha rose and said, "Hear the word of the Lord; to-morrow about this time a measure of fine flour and two measures of barley shall be sold for a piece of silver in the city gate." The nobleman on whose hand the king leaned answered, "If the Lord were to make windows in heaven, might this thing be?" and Elisha turned to him, and said, "You shall see it with your eyes, but shall not eat of it."

CHAPTER CXLIX
THE EMPTY CAMP

THAT evening four beggar men who sat in the city gate said to one another, "Why do we sit here till we die of hunger? Let us go to the camp of the Syrians; if they give us food we shall live, and if they kill us, we shall but die." So at dusk they rose and went out; but when they reached the camp, they found it empty, with the horses tied and the tents as they were, but no man to be seen. For God had made the Syrians hear a noise in the dusk as of chariots and horses and a great host, so that they thought that the kings of the Hittites and the kings of the Egyptians had been hired by the king of Israel and were marching against them; and in the twilight, leaving their tents and horses and the camp as it was, they had fled for their life. The four beggar men went into a tent, and ate and drank, and finding silver and gold and clothes in it, took them away and hid them, and then went on to another tent and did the same there. At last they said to one another, "If we loiter here till morning light, some mischief will come upon us; let us go and tell the king's household." So they went back and called to the sentinels at the city-gate and told them in what case they had found the camp. The sentinels called up the king's house; and the king rose in the night and said to his servants, "I will tell you what the Syrians have done. They know that we are starving; therefore they have left their camp and hidden themselves in the field, that when we come out they may fall upon us suddenly and break into the city." Then some one advised that they should send four or five men and horses to see; so they harnessed two chariots and went after the Syrians as far as Jordan, and found all the road full of clothes and arms that they had dropped in their flight. At daybreak they returned and told the king; then the gates were opened and the people rushed out to plunder the camp; and that day a measure of flour and two measures of barley were sold for a piece of silver in the gate. But the king appointed the nobleman on whose hand he leaned, and who had asked how such a thing might be, to have charge at the gate; and the crowd rushing through the gate knocked him down and trod on him, and he died; so he saw the plenty with his eyes, but did not eat of it.

CHAPTER CL
THE ARROWS OF KING JORAM

WHEN Elisha lay very sick and near his death, the king of Israel came to visit him, and wept over his face, saying, "O my father, my father, the chariot and horsemen of Israel!" The sick man said to the king, "Take your bow and arrows." The king took them; then he said, "Draw the bow." The king drew it; and Elisha laid his hands upon the king's hands, and said, "Open the east window;" and when they had opened it, he said to the king, "Shoot." The king shot through the window; and Elisha cried, "The arrow of the Lord's deliverance!" Then he said to the king, "Take the sheaf of arrows, and strike with them on the ground." The king took them, and struck them on the ground thrice, and stopped. Then Elisha said, "You should have struck five or six times; then you would have smitten the Syrians till you had destroyed them; now you shall smite them but thrice;" and when he had said this, he died.

CHAPTER CLI
THE MUTINY OF THE CAPTAINS

KING Joram went out to war against the Syrians, and won three battles over them; but afterwards he lost all his battles, and was wounded and went home to be healed; and while he lay sick at Jezreel, his sister's son, the young king Ahaziah of Judah, came to visit him. Meanwhile his captains began to mutiny against him; and a prophet came to the army at Ramoth-Gilead, where the captains were sitting in a room together, and said to Jehu the son of Nimshi, "I have an errand to you, O captain." So they went into another room; and there the prophet poured a vial of oil on his head, saying, "The Lord anoints you king over Israel," and then opened the door and fled away. When Jehu came out after him, the other captains asked, "Why did this mad fellow come to you?" He told them; and they all spread their cloaks under him at the top of the staircase, and proclaimed him king with sound of trumpets. Then Jehu ordered that the gates should be shut, and no news allowed to go forth of the city; and he harnessed his chariot and rode straight to Jezreel as fast as he could go.

CHAPTER CLII
THE RIDE FROM RAMOTH-GILEAD

AT the palace in Jezreel the watchman on the tower saw him coming in the distance, and called down to king Joram, "I see a company." Joram ordered the horseman who was on guard at the palace gate to gallop out and meet them and ask, "Is it peace?" But when he rode up and cried, "Is it peace?" Jehu answered, "What have you to do with peace? Turn and ride behind me." The watchman on the tower looked, and told the king, "The messenger has met them, but he does not come back." Then the king sent out a second horseman with the same message; and presently the watchman cried from the tower, "They have met, but he does not come back; and the driving is like the driving of Jehu the son of Nimshi; for he drives furiously." King Joram said, "Harness!" and he and his nephew, king

Ahaziah of Judah, rode out each in his own chariot; but they were hardly out of the palace when they met Jehu in the field of Naboth the Jezreelite. When they came near, Joram cried, "Is it peace, Jehu?" Jehu answered, " What peace, so long as your mother, Jezebel the sorceress, is alive?" King Joram turned rein, crying to the king of Judah, "Treachery, O Ahaziah!" but as he turned, Jehu drew his bow and shot; and the arrow struck Joram between the shoulders and went out through his heart, and he fell dead on his face in the chariot. Then Jehu said to his squire, "Take him up, and cast him in the field of Naboth; for remember, how when I and you rode together behind Ahab his father, the Lord laid this burden on him, saying, Surely I have seen the blood of Naboth and of his children, and I will make repayment in this field."

CHAPTER CLIII
THE WINDOW OVER THE GATE

MEANWHILE the king of Judah had fled by the way of the garden house; but Jehu pursued him, and within a little way overtook him and killed him in his chariot; then he turned and rode back to Jezreel. When Queen Jezebel heard the cry that her son was dead, she had put on her richest dress and crowned herself and painted her eyes, and sat in the window above the gate; and as Jehu rode in at the gate below, she leaned over the window, and said, "Had Zimri peace, who slew his master?" Jehu only looked up at the window and said, "Who is on my side?" Two or three servants of the royal household looked out to him, and he said, "Throw her down." So they threw her down into the street, and he trod her under his feet as he went into the palace. There he ate and drank, and then said, "Go now to this cursed woman and bury her, for she is a king's daughter." But when they went to bury her they found that the dogs had eaten her under the wall, and nothing was left of her but her skull and the bones of her feet and hands. So the house of Ahab was destroyed, and Jehu reigned over Israel.

CHAPTER CLIV
THE STORY OF THE CEDAR AND THE THISTLE

AFTER Jehu, his son Joash became king of Israel; and king Amaziah of Judah, who had won a great victory over the Edomites in the Valley of Salt, sent to challenge Joash to battle. Joash sent this message back: "The thistle that was in Lebanon sent to the cedar that was in Lebanon, saying, Give thy daughter to my son to wife; and the wild beast that was in Lebanon passed by, and trod down the thistle. You have indeed smitten Edom, and your heart has lifted you up; glory over this and tarry at home; for why should you meddle to your hurt, and fall, even you and all Judah with you?" But the king of Judah would not listen to counsel; therefore the king of Israel went out to war, and the two kings met in battle at the House of the Sun. The king of Israel defeated the king of Judah and took him prisoner; then he marched to Jerusalem and broke down the city wall and took away all the treasures in the temple and palace, and returned to Samaria.

CHAPTER CLV
THE ASSYRIAN CAPTIVITY

BUT the king of Judah sent for help to the king of Assyria in Nineveh; and soon the king of Assyria came from Nineveh with a great army and took Samaria after a three years' siege and carried the inhabitants away captive into Media, and repeopled the land from Babylonia and Susiana; so there was an end of the kingdom of Israel and of ten out of the twelve tribes, and the kingdom of Judah was left alone. But when the ten tribes were carried away captive, they took counsel among themselves to go forth into a further country; so they crossed Euphrates by the narrow passages of the river (for the Most High held still the flood till they had passed over) and went a great way into the mountains of the East; there they lived waiting for the Most High to stay the springs of the river again and let them pass through, when the time should come for them to return into their own land; and the story tells no more of them.

CHAPTER CLVI
THE TEMPEST

WHEN the kingdom of Nineveh ruled all the East, the word of the Lord came to the prophet Jonah bidding him go and prophesy against it. But he did not wish to go; so he went down to the seaport of Joppa, and there finding a ship in harbour ready to sail for Spain, he paid his fare and got on board to go with them to Spain away from the presence of the Lord. Soon after they had set sail the wind rose, and there was a great tempest. The sailors were afraid that their ship would be dashed to pieces; they cried each to his god, and lightened the ship by throwing their wares overboard into the sea. But Jonah had gone below and lay fast asleep, till the captain came and awoke him, saying, " What do you mean, sleeper? Rise, and call upon God, that we perish not." Then all the crew cast lots to know for whose cause they were in trouble; and the lot fell upon Jonah. They asked him who and whence he was and what was his occupation; and when he told them how he was a prophet and had fled from the presence of the Lord, they said, "What shall we do, that the sea may be calm for us?" for the sea grew more and more, and though they rowed hard they could not bring the ship to land. He said, "Take me up and cast me forth into the sea; for this great tempest is upon you for my sake." So they took him up and threw him into the sea, and immediately it grew calm. But God had prepared a great fish to swallow Jonah; and he was in the belly of the fish three days and three nights; then God spoke to the fish, and it vomited him out upon dry land.

CHAPTER CLVII
JONAH'S GOURD

THEN the word of the Lord came to Jonah a second time, bidding him go to Nineveh and deliver his message; so he rose and went. Now Nineveh was a very great city, three days' journey from end to end; and Jonah went a day's journey into it, crying aloud as he went, "Yet forty days and Nineveh shall be overthrown." When the cry spread, and reached the King of Nineveh in his palace, he came down from his throne and put off his royal robes and dressed himself in sackcloth; and he proclaimed throughout the city that all the people should fast and pray and leave off all their wickedness, that God might have mercy. Then God had mercy on them, and did not destroy the city; but Jonah was exceedingly angry, and cried to God, "O Lord, was not this why I fled away from thy presence? for I knew thee for a gracious God, slow to anger and of great kindness. Take away my life, I beseech thee, for I had rather die than live." But God said, "Do you well to be angry?" Now Jonah had gone out of Nineveh and sat on the east side of the city in a booth that he had made for shelter from the sun, waiting to see what would become of the city; and God prepared a gourd which grew over the booth and kept it cool with the shadow of its leaves, so that Jonah was glad because of the gourd. But early next morning God prepared a worm that ate into the gourd, and it withered; then God prepared a fierce east wind, and all day the sun beat upon Jonah till he grew faint, and was so sorry for himself and for the gourd that he said, "I wish I were dead." Then God said, "You have had pity on the gourd, for which you did not labour to make it grow, which came up in a night and perished in a night; and should not I have pity on Nineveh, that great city, wherein are more than six score thousand children too young to know their right hand from their left, and also much cattle?"

CHAPTER CLVIII
THE DESTROYING ANGEL

IN the reign of Hezekiah king of Judah, Sennacherib king of Assyria came with his army against Judah and took their fortresses and prepared to lay siege to Jerusalem: but first he sent three of his captains to summon it to surrender. They rode up to the city gate and called aloud to the king and all the people on the wall in these words: "Thus saith the great king, the king of Assyria; make peace with me, O people, and surrender your city, and eat every man of his own vine and fig-tree and drink every one of his own well, until I come and take you away to another land, a land of corn and wine, a land of bread and vineyards, a land of oil-olive and honey, that you may live and not die. Do not be deceived and think that the Lord will deliver you. Has any one of the gods of the nations delivered his country out of my hand? where are the kings of Hamath and Arpad? where are the kings of Sepharvaim, Hena, and Ivah, or the children of Eden in Telassar? The feet of my armies have dried up the rivers of besieged places, and made walled cities into ruinous heaps." But the prophet Isaiah said to the king of Judah, " Do not be afraid; for the Lord shall send a blast upon him, and he shall hear a rumour, and return home by the way he came, and fall by the sword in his own land." That same night the angel of the Lord went out and smote the camp of the Assyrians, and when they rose early in the morning, a hundred and eighty-five thousand men lay dead in the camp. So Sennacherib and the remnant of his army returned with shame to Nineveh ; and there two of his own sons killed him as he worshipped in a temple, and fled out of the land. But King Hezekiah had riches and honour, and made himself treasuries for silver and gold and pleasant jewels, and storehouses for corn and wine and oil, and stalls for cattle and cotes for flocks; and when he was sick, God added fifteen years to his life, and for a sign made the shadow on the sundial go ten degrees backward; and there was peace and truth in his days.

CHAPTER CLIX
THE GRAVEYARD ON THE HILL

JOSIAH king of Judah put down all the worshippers of strange gods in his land, and those who burned incense to the sun and moon and the host of heaven; he took away the horses that the kings of Judah had given to the sun, which were stalled in the cloisters of the temple, and burned the chariots of the sun with fire, and broke down the altars of the sun and moon that stood on the palace roof, and the high place of Moloch and Ashtaroth that king Solomon had built on the hill. Then he went to Bethel, and broke down the altar that Jeroboam king of Israel had made there for the worship of the golden calf, and as he turned he saw the tombs of the priests of the golden calf, that were on the hill, and took the bones out of them and burned them on the altar. Then he said, " Whose tombstone is that I see yonder?" The people of the place told him, "It is the tomb of the man of God out of Judah who foretold the things that are being done to-day." The king said, "Let him alone; let no one move his bones." So his bones, and the bones of the old prophet who was buried beside him, were left at peace in their tomb.

CHAPTER CLX
THE WATERS OF BABYLON

WHEN Cyaxares king of Media and Nabopolassar king of Babylon had besieged Nineveh and taken it, they broke down the fifty miles of wall and the fifteen hundred towers, and burned all the city, leaving it a vast wilderness of ruins; then the kingdom of Babylon grew great and began to conquer all the other kingdoms of the East. Pharaoh-Necho king of Egypt marched with an army against the king of Babylon, but was conquered in a great battle at Carchemish on the Euphrates. After that battle the kingdom of Judah became vassal to Babylon; and when it rebelled, Nebuchadnezzar king of Babylon came with his army and took Jerusalem by storm after a siege of eighteen months. The king of Judah fled by night to escape into the desert, but was pursued and caught; and Nebuchadnezzar put out his eyes and bound him with fetters of brass and carried him away to Babylon. The captain of the royal guard remained behind at Jerusalem to break down the city walls and burn the Temple and the palace and all the great houses; and when this was done, he returned to Babylon, taking the most part of the people with him into captivity, and only leaving a few poor men as husbandmen and vinedressers. A governor and a small guard of Babylonian soldiers were left in garrison; but within a few months afterwards they were treacherously attacked and killed by a band of fugitives from Jerusalem; whereupon all the remnant of the people, fearing the anger of the king of Babylon when he came to hear of it, rose and fled into Egypt; and for seventy years after the land lay desolate and without inhabitants. But by the waters of Babylon the captive people hung their harps upon the willows, and wept as they remembered Zion.

CHAPTER CLXI
THE VISION OF THE CHERUBIM

IN the land of Babylon by the river Chebar the prophet saw a whirlwind come out of the north, like a fire unfolding itself, and in the middle of the fire was a brightness like amber, and four living creatures sparkling like burnished brass, each with four wings and four faces, and their wings were full of eyes. They went each one straight forward, not turning as they went, and ran and returned like the appearance of a flash of lightning. Then as he looked he saw beside them four wheels of the colour of chrysolite, all four in one likeness, so high that they were dreadful, and full of eyes. Their appearance was as it were a wheel in the middle of a wheel; and they went by the living creatures, going where they went and rising off the earth where they rose; for the soul of the living creatures was in the wheels. Over their heads was a canopy like the colour of the terrible crystal, and when they went he heard the noise of their wings which spoke; when they stood at rest they let down their wings, but still a voice came from the canopy over them, and cried in his hearing, " O WHEEL." Above the canopy that was over their heads was the likeness of a throne made of a sapphire, and upon the throne was the likeness of a man above upon it, shining like fire, with the brightness of a rainbow round about him. Then the prophet knew that the living creatures were the cherubim, and that what he saw above them was the appearance of the glory of God.

CHAPTER CLXII
THE VISION OF THE HORSES IN THE VALLEY

BY night in a vision the prophet saw a man riding on a red horse, who stood among the myrtle trees in a valley, and behind him were other horses, red, speckled, and white; and he said to the angel beside him, " O my lord, what are these ? " The angel answered, " These are they whom the Lord has sent to walk to and fro through the earth." Then the horses spoke to the angel that stood among the myrtle trees, saying, " We have walked to and fro through the earth, and lo, the whole earth sits still and is at rest;" and the angel cried to heaven, "O Lord of hosts, how long wilt thou not have mercy on Jerusalem, which has been desolate for seventy years?"

CHAPTER CLXIII
THE VISION OF THE GOLDEN LAMPS

THE angel came to the prophet and waked him as a man that is wakened out of sleep, and said, "What do you see?" Then he looked and saw a candlestick all of gold, with a bowl upon the top and seven lamps, and seven pipes from the bowl to the seven lamps, and two olive trees, one on the right and the other on the left, that kept pouring golden oil into the bowl; and he asked, "What are these, my lord?" The angel said, "These seven lamps are the eyes of the Lord, which run to and fro throughout the world; and these two olive-trees are the two Anointed Ones that stand by the Lord of the whole earth."

CHAPTER CLXIV
THE VISION OF THE FOUR CHARIOTS

THE prophet turned and lifted up his eyes and looked, and lo, four chariots came out from between two mountains of brass. The horses in the first chariot were red, in the second black, in the third white, and in the fourth bay. The black horses went out into the north country, and the white followed them; the bay horses went out into the south country; and the red horses sought to go to and fro across the earth. Then he asked the angel who talked with him, "What are these, my lord?" and he answered, "These are the four Spirits of the Heavens, which go forth from standing before the Lord of the whole world."

CHAPTER CLXV
THE COMPLAINT OF THE CAPTIVES IN BABYLON

WHEN the people were captive in Babylon and the holy city lay waste, they cried to God and said thus: "O Lord that bearest rule, of all the trees in every wood of the earth thou hast chosen for thyself one vine: and of all lands of the whole world thou hast chosen thee one garden: and of all the flowers in it one lily: and of all the depths of the sea thou hast filled thee one river; and of all builded cities thou hast hallowed Zion unto thyself. And of all the birds that are created thou hast named thee one dove: and of all the cattle that are made thou hast provided thee one lamb: and among all the multitude of peoples thou hast got thee one people: and unto this people whom thou lovedst thou hast given thy law. Now, O Lord, why hast thou given this thy one people over to the heathen? though thou didst hate them, yet shouldst thou punish them with thine own hands." But God answered: " In the beginning when the earth was made, before the winds blew, before the fair flowers were seen, before the innumerable multitudes of angels were gathered together, then I considered these things; through me and none other they were done, and by me and none other shall they be brought to an end."

CHAPTER CLXVI
THE VALLEY OF DRY BONES

THE hand of God carried out the prophet and set him down in a valley in the desert, that was full of men's bones, and made him pass by them; they lay thick over all the open valley, bleached and dry. The Spirit of God said to him, "Son of man, can these dry bones live?" He answered, "O Lord God, thou knowest." Then God said, "Prophesy upon these bones and bid them hear the word of the Lord." So he cried to them, "O ye dry bones, hear the word of the Lord;" and there was a noise and a shaking, and the bones came together, bone to bone; and even as he looked, the sinews and the flesh came up upon them and the skin covered them above; but there was no breath in them. Then God said, "Prophesy to the wind, prophesy, son of man, and say to the wind, Come from the four winds, O breath, and breathe upon these slain, that they may live." So he prophesied; and the breath came into them, and they lived and stood up on their feet, an exceeding great army.

CHAPTER CLXVII
THE MAGICIANS

NEBUCHADNEZZAR king of Babylon dreamed a dream by night that troubled him, so that he could not sleep; therefore he sent for all his magicians and astrologers and sorcerers to give him counsel. They came before him, and said, "O king, live for ever; tell us the dream and we will interpret it." Nebuchadnezzar answered, "Do you tell me what my dream was, and then I shall know that you are able to interpret it. If you do this, I will give you gifts and great honours; but if you do not, you shall be cut in pieces, and your houses be made a dunghill." The magicians were amazed, and said to him, "There is not a man upon earth that can do this, nor has any king ever asked such a thing of any astrologer; it is a rare thing that the king requires; except the gods whose dwelling is not with men, there is no other who can do it." But the king was very furious, and ordered the chief of the executioners to kill all the wise men of Babylon.

CHAPTER CLXVIII
THE WISDOM OF DANIEL

NOW among the magicians were four children, who had been chosen out of the captives from Judah to be brought up in the palace and taught wisdom and magic for three years, that they might stand before the king; their names were Daniel, Hananiah, Mishael and Azariah; and they had skill in all magic, and in visions and dreams. When the decree went forth to kill the wise men, Daniel went to the chief of the executioners and prevailed on him to delay it for a day, "and to-morrow," he said, "I myself will tell the king his dream." Then he and the other three children all prayed to God, and God revealed the secret to Daniel in a vision at night. In the morning he awoke and gave thanks to God, and went to the chief of the executioners, who was making ready to kill the magicians; and they went together to the king. Then Daniel stood before the king and said, "O king, as you lay in your bed you thought of what things should come to be after you; then you saw, and lo, a great image, bright and terrible, stood before you. The head of the image was of fine gold, the breast and arms of silver, the belly and thighs of brass, the legs of iron, and the feet partly of iron and partly of clay. You looked, and saw a stone cut out without hands, which struck the image on its feet of clay and iron, and broke them in pieces; then the clay, the iron, the brass, the silver and the gold all crumbled together and the wind blew them away, like chaff on a summer threshing-floor; but the stone became a great mountain, and filled all the earth. This was your dream, O king; and this is the interpretation of it: You, who rule over all the children of men in glory, are the head of gold. After you shall arise another kingdom, inferior to you, as silver is to gold; and after it a third kingdom of brass, which shall bear rule over all the earth; and then a fourth kingdom of iron, which shall break all things in pieces; and that kingdom shall be divided, and be partly strong and partly weak, like iron mixed with clay; then after it God shall set up a kingdom of his own which shall never be destroyed, but shall break in pieces all those other kingdoms, and shall stand for ever." When King Nebuchadnezzar heard his dream told him, he said to Daniel, "Truly your God is a God of Gods and a Lord of kings and a Revealer of secrets." So he spared the magicians, and made Daniel ruler over Babylon; then Daniel made request of the king, and he set the other three children over the affairs of the province; but Daniel sat in the gate of the king.

CHAPTER CLXIX
THE FIERY FURNACE

NEBUCHADNEZZAR the king made a golden image a hundred feet high, and set it up in the plain of Babylon. He sent for all the princes, governors, captains, and councillors of all the provinces of his kingdom to come to the dedication of the image; and a herald cried aloud: "O peoples, nations, and languages! it is commanded that at what time you hear the sound of the cornet, flute, harp, sackbut, psaltery, dulcimer, and all kinds of music, you shall fall down and worship the golden image; and whoever does not fall down and worship shall the same hour be cast into the middle of a burning fiery furnace." Then the music sounded, and all the people fell down and worshipped. But certain men of Babylon came to the king and said to him: "O king, live for ever; the three children whom you have set over the province of Babylon have not fallen down and worshipped your golden image." Nebuchadnezzar in his rage and fury commanded the three children to be brought before him and asked them, "What is this?" They answered, "O king, our God whom we serve is able to save us from the burning fiery furnace, and will deliver us from your hand; we will not worship your golden image." Then the king was full of fury; he commanded that the furnace should be heated seven times hotter than usual, and that the strongest men in his army should bind the three children and throw them in. So the furnace was heated with oil and pitch and small wood till the flames streamed out high into the air and no one could go near it for the heat; then the three children, in their coats and hats, just as they stood, were seized and bound and thrown into the furnace. The violent heat of the furnace made the men who threw them in fall down dead when they came near it; but the three children fell bound into the middle of the fire. But God kept the heat of the furnace off them, and it only burned the cords with which they were bound; and they stood up and walked in the midst of the fire, praising God, and singing, "O all ye works of the Lord, bless ye the Lord; praise Him, and magnify Him for ever." Nebuchadnezzar rose up in haste from his throne, and said to his court, "Did we not cast three men bound into the furnace?" They answered, "Yes, O king." He said, "Lo, I see four men loose, walking in the midst of the fire, and they have no hurt, and the form of the fourth is like the Son of God." Then he went as near as he might to the mouth of the furnace, and called to them to come out. They came out, and the king and all his court saw that there was not a hair of their head singed, nor were their coats discoloured, nor did they smell of burning. Then Nebuchadnezzar worshipped God, and promoted the three children in the province of Babylon.

CHAPTER CLXX
THE PROUD KING

KING Nebuchadnezzar walked on the roof of his palace, looking down from it upon the city, that lay for miles along both sides of the river with its temples and gardens and palaces and towers, and said to himself, "Is not this great Babylon, that I have built for the home of my kingdom, by the might of my power and for the honour of my majesty?" But while the words were in his mouth a voice fell from heaven, and said, "O king Nebuchadnezzar, the kingdom is taken from you, and they shall drive you from among men, and you shall live with the beasts of the field eating grass like oxen, until you know that the Most High rules, and gives the kingdom to whomsoever he will." Then the king's reason left him: he was deposed from his kingdom and driven from among men, and ate grass like an ox for seven years in the open field, until his hair grew like eagles' feathers and his nails like birds' claws. At the end of seven years his reason returned to him, and he knew what had come upon him and worshipped the Most High; and his councillors and lords came back to him and established him again in his kingdom.

CHAPTER CLXXI
THE WRITING ON THE WALL

BELSHAZZAR the king made a great feast to a thousand of his lords, and they drank out of the gold and silver vessels which his father Nebuchadnezzar had taken from the Temple in Jerusalem. While they sat drinking wine and praising their gods of gold and silver, the fingers of a man's hand came forth and wrote words upon the plaster of the wall of the banqueting-house, opposite the candles. The king saw the part of the hand that wrote, and his countenance was changed, and his knees knocked against one another with fear. He called for all the astrologers and magicians, and said, "Whoever shall read this writing and interpret it shall be clothed with scarlet, and wear a chain of gold about his neck, and be one of the three rulers of the kingdom." But none of them could read it or interpret it. The rumour spread over all the palace; and the king's mother came into the banqueting-house, and said, "O king, live for ever: there is a man in your kingdom called Daniel, in whom is the spirit of the holy gods, and your father Nebuchadnezzar made him his master of the magicians for his excellence in interpreting dreams and dissolving doubts and shewing hard sentences; let him be called, and he shall interpret it." Then the king sent for Daniel; and he came in and said; "O king, God gave your father a great kingdom, so that all nations trembled before him; but when his heart was lifted up with pride, his glory was taken away from him and he was made like a wild beast, eating grass and wet with the dew of heaven, until he knew that God rules in the kingdoms of men. Yet you his son have not humbled your heart, but have drunk wine in the vessels of the house of the High Lord, praising your idols of silver and gold, and not giving glory to God in whose hand your breath is. The writing that is written on the wall is this, MENE, MENE, TEKEL, UPHARSIN: that is to say, NUMBERED, NUMBERED, WEIGHED, AND DIVIDED. And the interpretation of it is this: God has numbered your kingdom and finished it; you are weighed in the balances and found wanting; and your kingdom is divided and given to the Medes and Persians." Then king Belshazzar commanded to clothe Daniel in scarlet, and put a chain of gold about his neck, and proclaim him one of the three rulers of the kingdom. But that same night the Median and Persian army under Darius king of Media broke into Babylon by the dry bed of the river, and killed Belshazzar in his palace and brought the Babylonian empire to an end.

CHAPTER CLXXII
THE DEN OF LIONS

KING Darius set over his empire a hundred and twenty princes, one over each province; but he honoured Daniel above them all, and meditated to set him over the whole kingdom. The princes were jealous, and plotted against Daniel, but could find no occasion to accuse him to the king. At last they came all together to the king and said, "King Darius, live for ever: all the presidents, governors, princes, councillors and captains of your kingdom have consulted together, and advise you to make a law, that whoever shall ask a petition for the next thirty days of any god or man, except of the king, shall be thrown the same day into the den of lions." Then the king signed the decree. But when Daniel knew that this law was made, he went into his house, and leaving his windows open towards Jerusalem, he kneeled down and prayed to God as he always did thrice a day. His enemies watched him, and then went to the king, and said, "O king, that man Daniel, who is one of the captives from Judah, does not obey your decree, but prays to his God three times a day." The king was very angry with himself, and laboured all the rest of the day to save him, but could find no way of escape; for it was the law of the Medes and Persians that no decree of the king might be changed. So at sunset Daniel was thrown into the den of lions and a stone laid on the mouth of the den, which the king and his lords sealed with their own signets, that no man might move it. The king went back to his palace in great displeasure, and had no music played to him, and did not eat or sleep all night. Very early in the morning he rose and went in haste to the den of lions, and cried with a lamentable voice into the den, "O Daniel, has your God delivered you from the lions?" A voice came back out of the den: "O king, live for ever: my God has sent his angel and shut the lions' mouths, so that they have not hurt me." The king was very glad, and commanded his servants to take Daniel up out of the den; but the men who had accused him were brought and thrown into the den instead of him; and the lions had the mastery of them, and broke all their bones in pieces before ever they reached the bottom of the den.

CHAPTER CLXXIII
THE FEAST IN THE PALACE OF THE LILY

AHASUERUS king of Persia, who reigned from India to Africa over a hundred and twenty-seven provinces, made a feast in his Palace of the Lily to all his people both great and small, and they drank royal wine in abundance from cups of gold in the garden-court of the palace, which was paved with marble and alabaster and mother-of-pearl, and covered from the sun with canopies of white, green, and blue. On the seventh day of the feast, being merry with wine King Ahasuerus commanded his seven chamberlains to bring out Vashti the Queen in her royal robes, that the princes and people might look on her; for she was very beautiful. But Vashti was so proud, that she refused to come at his bidding; therefore the king decreed that she should be removed from her royal estate and that another queen should be chosen instead of her. Officers were sent through all the provinces of the kingdom to choose the most beautiful women that could be found and bring them to the palace, that a queen might be taken from among them; and one of those who were chosen was a Jewess called Esther, who was one of the captives in Babylon. Her father and mother were dead, and her cousin Mordecai, who sat in the gate of the Palace of the Lily, had brought her up. She was brought to the palace and given in charge to the keeper of the women; and he was pleased with her, and gave her dresses and ornaments and seven maids to wait on her; and when her turn came to go before the king, she found favour with him more than all the other women; so he set the royal crown on her head, and made her queen instead of Vashti; but she kept it secret that she belonged to the people of the Jews.

CHAPTER CLXXIV
THE MALICE OF HAMAN

ABOUT this time two of the royal chamberlains laid a plot to kill the king, which came to the ears of Mordecai, as he sat in the palace gate. He sent word of it to his cousin, Queen Esther, and she told the king; then the two chamberlains were tried and hanged, and the account of the trial was written in the book of the chronicles of the kingdom. Afterwards the king promoted one of his servants called Haman to great honour, and made him a prince; and all the king's servants in the palace bowed to him, except Mordecai, who would not bow to him because Haman was an enemy of the Jews. Then Haman was full of anger, and thought it a small thing to punish Mordecai alone, but determined to take revenge on all the Jews throughout the kingdom. He went to the king and said, "There is a certain people scattered and dispersed in all the provinces of your kingdom, who do not keep your laws; and it is not for your profit to endure them. If it please the king, let them be destroyed; the cost will be ten thousand talents of silver, but I will pay for it." The king consented, and taking the signet ring from his finger, gave it to Haman that the thing might be done. So the king's secretaries were set to write copies of a letter in all the languages of the kingdom, written in the king's name, and sealed with his ring, and it was sent out by posts to all the governors of the provinces, ordering them to destroy and kill all Jews, young and old, women and little children, upon one day, namely, the thirteenth day of the twelfth month. Then the king and Haman sat down to drink; but the City of the Lily was perplexed.

CHAPTER CLXXV
THE GOLDEN SCEPTRE

THERE was great terror among the Jews; and Mordecai sent a copy of the decree to Queen Esther, and told her that she must go to the king and make supplication for her people. She sent him answer, "All men know that whoever comes before the king into the inner court of the palace without being called for is put to death, unless the king holds out his golden sceptre to him that he may live; and for the last thirty days I have not been called for to go in to the king." He sent back word again, "Do not think to escape yourself, when all your people perish; nay, if you fail us now, deliverance shall come from elsewhere, and you and your family be destroyed; and who knows but it was for this that you were chosen queen?" Then Esther returned answer, "Gather all the Jews in the city, and fast and pray for me for three days, night and day, and I will go to the king; and if I perish, I perish." At the end of three days she put on her royal robes, and went and stood in the gate of the inner court opposite the king as he sat on his throne. When the king saw her, she was pleasing in his sight, and he held out the golden sceptre to her and said, "What is your desire, Queen Esther? it shall be given you, even to the half of the kingdom." She answered, "May it please the king to come to-day with Haman to a banquet that I have prepared for him." So they came to the banquet; and there the king again bade her name her desire. She answered, "If I have found favour in the king's sight, let the king and Haman come again to my banquet to-morrow, and then I will make my request." Haman went home from the banquet joyfully, and calling his wife and all his friends, told them of his riches and glory and how the king had promoted him above all the princes of the kingdom; "Yes, and to-day," he said, "when the queen invited the king to a banquet, I was the only other person invited, and to-morrow I am to go again: yet all this avails me nothing, so long as I see Mordecai the Jew, who refuses to do me reverence, sitting in the palace gate." His wife and his friends said to him, "Let a gallows be built eighty feet high, and to-morrow morning speak to the king that Mordecai may be hanged on it; then you can go merrily to the queen's banquet." The advice pleased Haman, and he had the gallows built.

CHAPTER CLXXVI
THE BOOK OF THE CHRONICLES OF THE KINGDOM

THAT night the king could not sleep; so the book of the chronicles of the kingdom was brought and read out to him. There it was found written how Mordecai had discovered the conspiracy of the two chamberlains; and when the king asked what reward had been given him, it was found there had been none. By this time it was morning; and Haman was in the outer court of the palace waiting for an audience, that he might speak to the king to have Mordecai hanged. So when the king asked, "Who is in waiting?" they said, "Haman stands in the court." "Let him come in," said the king. Haman came in, and the king at once asked him, "What shall be done to the man whom the king delights to honour?" He thought within himself, "Whom should the king desire to honour but me?" so he considered, and then answered, "For the man whom the king delights to honour, let him be dressed in the royal robes and crown, and let one of the princes lead him riding on the king's own horse through the street of the city, proclaiming before him, Thus shall it be done to the man whom the king delights to honour." The king said to him, "Make haste, and take my robes and my horse, and do even as you have said to Mordecai the Jew, who sits in my gate." So Haman took Mordecai and arrayed him and brought him on horseback through the city, and then hastened home in grief, with his face covered, to tell his wife and friends what had happened. They said, "This promises badly for you;" and while they were still talking, and gave him but small comfort, a messenger from the palace came to say that the king waited for him to go to the banquet in the queen's pavilion.

CHAPTER CLXXVII
THE BANQUET IN THE QUEEN'S PAVILION

SO the king and Haman came to the queen's banquet; and there the king said again, "What is your desire, Queen Esther? it shall be done, even to the half of the kingdom." Then Esther rose, and fell at the king's feet, and answered, "If it please the king, let my life be given me; for I and my people are sold to be slain and to perish." "Who and where is he," said the king, "who dares presume to do this?" She answered, "The enemy is this wicked Haman." The king rose up from the table in a fury and went into the palace garden; and Haman fell down before Esther to plead with her for his life. He was lying across the queen's couch at her feet, when the king came back out of the garden into the pavilion. "Will he force the queen also in my house before my eyes?" cried the king; and as the words went out of the king's mouth, the attendants covered Haman's face. Then one of the chamberlains who waited on the king said, "See also, the gallows eighty feet high that this man had built for Mordecai, who saved the king's life, stands in his house." "Hang him on it," said the king; and he was hurried away and hanged.

CHAPTER CLXXVIII
THE RIDING OF THE POSTS

THEN king Ahasuerus took his signet ring, which he had taken away from Haman, and gave it to Mordecai the Jew; and letters were written from the Palace of the Lily in the king's name and sealed with his ring, to the governors of all the hundred and twenty-seven provinces between India and Africa, in the language of every people, and sent by royal posts on swift horses and camels and dromedaries, granting leave to the Jews to gather together and defend themselves against all men who attempted to do them harm on the thirteenth day of the twelfth month, which was the day that Haman had appointed for their destruction. So when the day came, no one dared to touch them; and on the fourteenth day of the month they were glad together, and kept the day as a festival. Then there was peace upon the people of Israel throughout all the realm of the king.

CHAPTER CLXXIX
THE RETURN FROM BABYLON

WHEN the people of God had been captives for seventy years in Babylon, Cyrus the Persian, king of kings, decreed that the temple of God at Jerusalem should be rebuilt, and that all who wished might go back and live again in the land of Judah, which had lain waste and kept Sabbath since the king of Babylon had taken the people away. Then many people returned, and lived in the old land of their fathers under a prince of the house of David; and as soon as they were settled in the land, they began to rebuild the temple. At the laying of the foundation-stone the trumpets sounded and the priests sang together, "Praise the Lord, because he is good, for his mercy endureth for ever," and the people shouted with a great shout of joy. But many of the ancient men, who had seen the first Temple in its glory, wept aloud; so that the noise of the shouting and weeping was heard far off.

CHAPTER CLXXX
THE RUINS AT NIGHT

AFTER they had built the second Temple, the walls and palaces of the city still lay in ruins where they had been broken down and burned. Word of this came to Nehemiah the Jew, who was cupbearer to king Artaxerxes in the Palace of the Lily; then he was very sad, so that the king asked what ailed him. "O king," he said, "why should not my face be sad, when the city of my fathers lies waste? please you send me there, that I may build it." So the king made him governor of Jerusalem, and sent him to rebuild the city. When he came to Jerusalem, he said nothing at first of what he had come to do; but at night he rose and mounted his horse quietly, and rode out by the valley gate and the dragon well. He rode outside the broken walls till he came to the fountain gate, and there his horse could not pass further among the rubbish heaps of the broken wall; so he climbed up the side of the valley in the dim light and viewed the wall, and then turning back, rode in again by the valley gate before break of day.

CHAPTER CLXXXI
THE BUILDING OF THE WALL

WHEN day came, Nehemiah called the nobles and rulers and told them his commission from the king; and all the people joyfully rose up at once and began to build the wall. Beginning at the sheep gate they built to the fish gate; and so by the broad wall and the tower of the furnaces to the valley gate; and from the fountain gate they built the wall by the king's garden and the stairs that go down from the castle, as far as the tower lying out from the king's high house by the court of the prison and so from the water gate by the great tower to the horse gate, and back to the sheep gate where they had begun. Every man built with his sword buckled on for fear of enemies, working from daybreak till the stars appeared at night; and the governor's guard patrolled the works night and day. So they never ceased till they had finished building the walls and gates, and the city was safe against enemies; and then they began to restore the palaces of the city and to renew it and make it fair as it had been in the ancient days.

CHAPTER CLXXXII
THE HEATHEN HOST

THE king of the heathen called for Holofernes the chief captain of his army, and said to him, "Go forth from my presence into the west with an army, and bid the nations of the west give me earth and water, and become my subjects; and if they do not yield themselves, put them to the slaughter and spare none." So Holofernes and his army went over Euphrates and destroyed all the high cities as far as the sea, and pitched his camp near the town of Bethulia, preparing to march into Judea. Then the high priest in Jerusalem wrote to Chabris and Charmis, the governors of Bethulia, to shut the passes of the hill country and fortify their town strongly against Holofernes, to keep him from entering the land. When Holofernes saw them preparing to resist him, he marched his army into the valley below Bethulia and took the fountains from which the town drew its water; but the townsmen kept him from coming further by slinging stones from the top of the hill, and kindled fires on the city towers and kept watch all night. Then the captains of the heathen army counselled Holofernes, "Do not assault the town, but keep the fountains in the valley, from which they get all their water, and wait until they are forced by thirst to surrender; for so you will win the city without losing any of your own men." This advice was taken; and the army besieged Bethulia for thirty days, till all the cisterns in it were empty, and men and women fainted and fell down in the streets for thirst, and had no strength any longer; and at last the people cried to the governor to surrender before they were all dead. He encouraged them to endure for five days more; and then, if no help came, he promised to give up the town.

CHAPTER CLXXXIII
THE VALOUR OF JUDITH

THERE was a young widow called Judith in Bethulia, whose husband had died three years before of a sunstroke in the field at barley harvest; she was very beautiful, and her husband had left her great wealth, and no one gave her an ill word. She sent for the governors of the city, and said to them, "What is this that you have done? God has power to save us or destroy us every day, and is not as a man who threatens or who wavers, that we should bind him down to five days; let us wait for his salvation till it please him." They answered, "The people compelled us to do this, and to take an oath to it, which we may not break." Then she said, "Hear me, and I will do a thing which shall be told of throughout all ages. Let me go forth to-night with my waiting-woman, and within the five days God shall deliver us by my hand." They answered, " Go, in God's name." At the hour when the evening incense was burned in the house of God at Jerusalem she prayed, and put off her mourning that she had worn ever since her husband died, and washed and anointed herself, and braided her hair, and put on her garments of gladness and her bracelets and chains and rings and all her ornaments; and she and her maid went to the city gate, where Chabris and Charmis, the ancients of the city, stood on guard. When they saw her, they wondered at her beauty, and opened the gates for her; and she and her maid went out, the men of the city looking after her as she went down the hill till the darkness hid her from sight.

CHAPTER CLXXXIV
THE SUPPER IN THE TENT

JUDITH went straight on till she met the sentinels of the enemy, and asked to be taken before their general; so they took her through the camp to Holofernes' tent. He came out of his tent with silver lamps going before him, and when he saw Judith, he was amazed at her beauty. She bowed down to the ground before him, and said, " My lord, the people of Bethulia fail of food and water, and have determined to consume things that the law of God forbids them to eat. Now you cannot prevail against them until they sin and provoke God; but when once they have sinned they will have no more power to resist you. Knowing this, I have fled from among them; and I will watch here in your camp and tell you as soon as they have sinned, that you may fall on them and destroy them." Holofernes was so charmed that he believed all she said, and she stayed in the camp three days; and each night the sentinels had orders to let her pass out between midnight and morning that she might pray by a fountain in the valley. On the evening of the fourth day Holofernes made a banquet in his tent, and sent for Judith. She put on all her ornaments, and her maid laid soft cushions for her on the ground in Holofernes' tent; then they ate and drank together, and Holofernes took great delight in her company, and drank more wine than he ever had drunk in his life before. When it grew late, the servants withdrew and went to bed; for they were all weary, because the feast had been long; and Judith was left alone with Holofernes, who by this time was heavy with wine, and lay along on his bed under a canopy woven with purple and gold and emeralds.

CHAPTER CLXXXV
THE HEAD OF HOLOFERNES

THEN Judith rose and took down his sword where it hung on the pillar of his bed, and catching him by the hair with her left hand, struck him twice on the neck with all her strength and cut off his head from his body. She tumbled his body from the bed and tore down the canopy over it, and came out of the tent carrying his head. Her maid, who was waiting for her outside, put it in a bag, and they passed out of the camp between midnight and morning as they had done before. But when they reached the fountain they went straight on, and took the way up the hill to Bethulia; and Judith called from far off to the watchmen at the gates, "Open, open! God is with us." They ran together and opened the gate by torchlight, and Judith cried, " Praise, praise God, praise God, for he hath not taken away his mercy from Israel!" Then she shewed them the head of Holofernes, and they were astonished. But as soon as it was morning, they hung out the head on the highest place of the city wall, and sallied forth against the enemy. The heathen captains came to the tent of Holofernes to awake him, that he might order the army for battle; but when they knocked and had no answer, one went in, and found the headless body lying on the floor. A cry and confusion rose throughout the camp, and the whole army broke up and fled; and the people of Bethulia chased them with great slaughter beyond Damascus. Judith lived many years in great honour; and many a man desired her to be his wife, yet she never married again, but grew old in her own house, and when she died she was buried in her husband's grave in Bethulia; and no one made the children of Israel afraid in her days, or for a long time after her death.

CHAPTER CLXXXVI
THE ERRAND OF THE ARCHANGEL

AMONG the children of Israel who were carried captive to Nineveh, was one Tobit of Thisbe, with his wife Anna and their son Tobias. He was a good man, who fed the hungry and clothed the naked, and buried the innocent people who had been killed by the heathen and their bodies thrown out behind the walls of Nineveh. But because he did these good deeds, all that he had was taken away from him by the king of Nineveh; also he became blind; so that they were very poor, and had nothing to live upon but what Anna earned by spinning. At that same time there lived at Ecbatana in Media one Raguel, who was Tobit's cousin; he had a daughter called Sara, a fair maid, who had been betrothed to seven husbands one after the other, but they all had been strangled by the evil spirit Asmodeus before they married her; so that her father's maid-servants mocked her, and she was ready to kill herself for grief and shame. Both these unhappy families prayed to God to take pity on them at the same time; and at the same time the prayer of both was heard, and God sent Raphael the archangel from his presence to help them in their trouble.

CHAPTER CLXXXVII
THE JOURNEY TO MEDIA

MANY years before this, Tobit had left ten talents of silver with a merchant in the city of Rages in Media, and now that he was poor he remembered it, and told his son Tobias that he must go to Rages and get it back. So Tobias went out into the market-place to seek a guide for the journey, and there he met the archangel Raphael in the dress of a guide. He said to him, "Can you go with me to Rages, and do you know that country well?" and Raphael answered, "Yes." So Tobias took him home to his father, who asked him his name. He said, "My name is Help-of-God, and I am one of your brethren." Then they agreed what wages Help-of-God should have, and got everything ready for the journey. When all was ready, Anna wept at parting with her son; but Tobit chid her, and said to Tobias, "Go now, and may God who dwells in heaven prosper your journey, and the angel of God keep you company." Then they started on their journey, and Tobias took his dog with him. At evening they came to an inn by the river, where they lodged for the night. Next morning, Tobias went down to bathe in the river, when a fish leaped out of the water at him. Raphael called from the bank to him, "Take the fish!" He caught it and pulled it to land, and Raphael told him to open it and take out the heart and liver and gall and put them up safely; then they roasted the fish and ate it, and went on their way, until they came to the city of Ecbatana. As they went, Tobias asked his companion, "Help-of-God, of what use are the heart and liver and gall of this fish?" and he answered, "If any one is troubled by a devil or an evil spirit, the smoke of the heart and liver will drive it away; and the gall rubbed on a blind man's eyes will make him see."

CHAPTER CLXXXVIII
THE FLIGHT OF THE EVIL SPIRIT

THEY went to Raguel's house in Ecbatana, who gave them welcome, and wept when he heard how his cousin Tobit was poor and blind. Now the angel had told Tobias on their journey of the fair maid Sara his cousin, and said, "I will speak to her father that you may marry her." "O brother Help-of-God," said Tobias, "I have heard that my cousin has been betrothed to seven men who all died in the marriage chamber, and I am afraid to marry her." The angel answered, "Have no fear, brother, for she was appointed to you from the beginning." So as they sat at supper, Tobias said, "Help-of-God, speak now about what you talked of on the way." Then Raphael opened the matter; but Raguel said, "It is fit that he should be her husband, for he is next of kin; but I will tell you the truth; seven men have died who wished to marry her." "I will eat nothing," said Tobias, "till you consent." So Raguel called Sara and took her by the hand and gave her to Tobias for his wife. At night when they were alone in the marriage chamber, Tobias took hot embers of spice, and laid some of the heart and liver of the fish upon them; and as soon as the evil spirit smelled the smoke, he fled away to prison in the furthest part of Egypt. Then they slept in peace; but Raguel had gone out alone in the dark and was digging a grave, that if Tobias were found dead in the morning they might bury him and no one know of it.

CHAPTER CLXXXIX
THE RETURN FROM ECBATANA

IN the morning when Tobias came out of his room alive and well, there was great joy in the house, and they filled up the grave, and held the wedding feast. Meanwhile Tobias sent Raphael with a servant and two camels to the city of Rages, where he received the bags of silver sealed up as Tobit had left them, and brought them back to Ecbatana. Then they set out on their journey home; and Raguel gave Sara half his wealth for her dowry; for she was his only child. When they were near Nineveh, the angel said to Tobias, "Let us hasten on before your wife and prepare the house; and take the gall of the fish in your hand." So they went on in front, and the dog ran after them. Tobit was sitting in his house, and his wife Anna sat by the door looking along the street for her son, when she saw them coming, and cried to Tobit, "Here he is, and the man who went with him." Anna ran out and fell upon her son's neck, and Tobit rose too, and was groping his way to the door, when Tobias ran to him, crying, "Be of good hope, my father;" and he rubbed the fish's gall on his father's eyes, and his sight came back to him. Then Tobias told him of all that had happened, and he went out to meet his daughter-in-law at the city gate, rejoicing and praising God.

CHAPTER CXC
THE WAGES OF RAPHAEL

THEN Tobit said to his son, "My son, see that the man who went with you have his wages, and you must give him more than was agreed." Tobias answered, "O my father, he deserves the half of all I have; for not only did he bring me safe home, but he drove away the evil spirit from my wife, and fetched me the money from Rages, and gave you back your sight." The old man said, "It is his due;" and he called the angel and said to him, "Take half of all that you and my son have brought, and go in peace." Then Raphael said to him, "It is good to keep close the secret of a king, but it is honourable to reveal the acts of God. When you prayed, and when Sara your daughter-in-law prayed in Media, I brought your prayers before the Holy One, and God sent me to help you; I am Raphael, one of the seven holy angels that go in and out before the glory of the Holiest. Now give God thanks, for I go up to him." Then he vanished out of their sight, and they worshipped God. Afterwards Tobit lived to a good old age; and he and his wife Anna died and were buried together ; then Tobias with his wife and children went to live at Ecbatana with Raguel, and there before he died he heard of the destruction of Nineveh.

CHAPTER CXCI
THE ANGEL OF ACCUSING

THERE was a man in the land of Uz whose name was Job ; he had seven thousand sheep and three thousand camels and five hundred yoke of oxen and five hundred she-asses, and a very great household, so that he was the greatest man in all the East ; and he had seven sons and three daughters. On a day, the angels all came to present themselves before God, and the Accusing Angel came among them. God said to him, "From whence come you ?" and he answered, "From going to and fro in the earth, and from walking up and down in it." God said, " Have you considered my servant Job, that there is none like him in the earth to fear God and do no evil ?" The Accusing Angel answered, and said, " Does Job fear God for nothing ? hast thou not made a hedge about him and about his house, and blessed the work of his hands, and increased his substance ? but put forth thine hand now and touch all that he has, and he will curse thee to thy face." God answered him, "Make trial; all that he has is in your power, but his own body." So the Angel of Accusing went forth from the presence of the Lord.

CHAPTER CXCII
THE FOUR MESSENGERS

ON a day, Job's sons and daughters were all together eating and drinking in their eldest brother's house, and Job sat alone at home, when a messenger came to him and said, "The oxen were ploughing and the asses feeding beside them, when the Sabeans fell upon them and took them away, and killed all the servants; I only have escaped to tell you." While he was speaking, another messenger came, and said, "Fire has fallen from heaven and burned up the sheep, and the shepherds with them; and I only have escaped to tell you." While the second messenger was speaking, yet another messenger came, and said, "Three bands of robbers fell upon the camels and have taken them away, and slain the servants with swords; and I only have escaped alone to tell you." While the third messenger was speaking, yet again another messenger came, and said, "Your sons and daughters were eating and drinking in their eldest brother's house, when a great wind from the wilderness came and smote the four corners of the house, so that it fell upon them, and they are dead; and I only have escaped alone to tell you." Then Job said, "The Lord gave and the Lord hath taken away; blessed be the name of the Lord."

CHAPTER CXCIII
THE PATIENCE OF JOB

THERE was a day again when the angels came to present themselves before God, and the Accusing Angel came among them; and God said to him, "From whence come you?" He answered, "From going to and fro in the earth, and from walking up and down in it." God said, "Have you considered my servant Job, that there is none like him in the earth to fear God and do no evil? and still he holds fast his goodness, though you have moved me to swallow him up without cause." The Accusing Angel answered and said, "All that a man has he will give for his life; but put forth thine hand now and touch his bone and his flesh, and he will curse thee to thy face." God answered him, "He is in your hand; all except his life." So the Angel of Accusing went out from the presence of God, and smote Job with sore boils from the sole of his foot to his crown. Then Job's wife said to him, "Do you still keep to your goodness? curse God, and die." But he said, "You speak as one of the foolish women speaks. What, shall we receive good at the hand of God, and shall we not receive evil?"

CHAPTER CXCIV
JOB'S COMFORTERS

WHEN Job's three friends, Eliphaz of the south, Bildad of the plain, and Zophar of the pleasant land, heard of all this evil that was come upon him, they made an appointment to go and see him, and comfort him. But when they came, he was so changed with his grief that they did not know him; and they lifted up their voice and wept, and rent their clothes and sprinkled dust upon their heads, and sat by him on the ground for seven days and seven nights without speaking to him. After this, Job opened his mouth and said, "Let the day perish whereon I was born. Wherefore is life given to him that is in misery, who longs for death, but it cometh not?" Eliphaz answered Job, and said, "Who ever perished, being innocent? Despise not the chastening of the Almighty. We have searched this out, and so it is; hear it, and know it for your good." But Job answered, "Teach me wherein I have erred, and I will hold my tongue; for my grief is heavier than the sand of the sea." Then Bildad said, "If you were pure and upright, surely you would be prosperous; God will not cast away the righteous." But Job answered, "It is all one; he destroyeth the perfect and the wicked; and he is not a man as I am, that we should come together in judgment." Then Zophar said, "If iniquity be in your hand, put it away, and you shall shine forth as the morning. Be sure that God exacts of you less than you deserve." But Job answered, "No doubt but you are the people, and wisdom shall die with you! Will you flatter God, and speak deceitfully for him? Let me alone, and let come on me what will; but though he slay me, yet will I trust in him, and declare the truth before him."

CHAPTER CXCV
THE PROSPERITY OF JOB

AT last Job's comforters ceased to answer him; and the Lord himself answered Job out of the whirlwind, saying, "Who is this that darkens counsel by words without knowledge? Will you condemn me, that you may be righteous?" Job answered the Lord, and said, "I know that thou canst do anything, and that no thought of thine can be hindered. I have uttered that which I understood not, and things too wonderful for me." Then the Lord said to Job's three friends, "My anger is kindled against you, because you have not spoken the truth of me, as my servant Job has; therefore make offerings to me and let my servant Job pray for you, lest I deal with you after your folly." So the Lord restored the prosperity of Job, and made him better off at the end than at the beginning; for he had fourteen thousand sheep, and six thousand camels, and a thousand yoke of oxen, and a thousand she-asses; he also had seven sons and three daughters, the fairest in all the land; and he saw his children's children, and died full of days.

CHAPTER CXCVI
THE MAN IN GOLDEN ARMOUR

AFTER Alexander son of Philip the Macedonian had reigned over all nations and kings for twelve years, he died, and his kingdoms were divided among his captains. At that time the holy city dwelt in peace, and kings honoured it and gave gifts to the temple. But when king Seleucus of Syria heard that the treasury at Jerusalem was full of infinite riches, he ordered his treasurer Heliodorus to plunder it, and bring him all the silver and gold that he found there. Heliodorus came to Jerusalem, and after being courteously received by the high priest, he told him his errand. There was great sorrow and commotion in the city; however, Heliodorus went into the temple to obey the king's orders. But as he and his guards were busy in the treasury, the apparition of a horse, with a very beautiful housing and a rider upon him in complete armour of gold, ran at him and struck him down with its forefeet; and he lay speechless, as if he were dead, till his guards carried him out on a litter. Then the high priest, fearing that the king might think some treachery had been done, prayed to God for him; and as he did so, two very beautiful young men dressed in splendid clothing stood by Heliodorus, and saying, "Give the high priest great thanks, since for his sake God has granted you your life," they disappeared out of sight. So Heliodorus returned to the king, and said to him, "If you have an enemy, or a traitor, send him on this business; for God defends that place with especial power, and destroys those who come to hurt it."

CHAPTER CXCVII
THE KING'S ELEPHANTS

AFTER king Seleucus was dead, his brother Antiochus reigned, and made war against the people of God. He entered forcibly into the temple, and took away the golden ornaments and the treasures, and set up the Abomination of Desolation upon the high altar. Then Mattathias the priest gathered an army and fought for Israel in the wilderness, till the time came for him to die, when he made his son Judas Maccabeus captain in his place. Judas fought against the heathen and won great victories and renown;

also he restored the desolate sanctuary, where the gates were burned, and the cloisters pulled down, and shrubs grew in the courts as in a forest; and he built up the castle of Zion with high walls and towers round about. Then the king sent a great army against him of a hundred and twenty thousand men, and thirty-two elephants trained to battle. Each elephant had a guard of five hundred horsemen, and carried on his back a strong tower with golden shields hung round it, and in the tower were thirty-two men who fought, besides the Indian who sat on the elephant's neck and guided him; and when the sun shone upon the golden shields they glittered like lamps of fire. But Judas Maccabeus gave them battle with three thousand men, and routed their army and cut it to pieces.

CHAPTER CXCVIII

THE WISDOM OF THE ROMANS

JUDAS MACCABEUS heard of the fame and valour of the Romans, and how they had subdued the Gauls, and what they had done in Spain to win the gold and silver mines; and how they had conquered by their policy and patience many lands that were very far off; and how they had overthrown Antiochus the Great, the king of Asia, when he fought against them with a great army and a hundred and twenty elephants, and how all men that heard their name were afraid of them; and how for all this none of them wore a crown or was clothed in purple, but they had made themselves a senate-house, in which three hundred and twenty men sat in council daily, consulting always for the good of the people. Therefore he sent ambassadors to Rome, and made alliance with the Senate and People of the Romans.

CHAPTER CXCIX
THE PEACE OF THE EMPIRE

SO Judas Maccabeus fought against the heathen and won many great victories, until at last he was killed in battle; and all Israel made great lamentation for him, and because of his noble acts and his valour he was counted among the Nine Worthies, with Joshua who led the people out of the wilderness into the promised land, and with David the King. But after his days the Romans took the country into their government; and it was a province of their empire when Octavianus Caesar Augustus the Emperor brought their civil wars to an end, and closed the gates of Janus in the City as a sign that the Peace of Rome was established over all the world. Then there was peace on earth while it waited for the Lord Jesus Christ to be born.

CHAPTER CC
THE VISION OF THE KINGDOM OF THE SAINTS

THE prophet saw in his vision by night how the four winds of heaven strove upon the great sea, and four great beasts came up out of the sea, diverse one from another. The first beast was like a lion, and had eagle's wings; the second beast was like a bear, and had three ribs in its mouth between its teeth, which said to it, "Arise, devour much flesh." The third beast was like a leopard, and had four wings on its back. The fourth beast was terrible and exceedingly strong, with great iron teeth; it devoured and broke in pieces and stamped with its feet; and it had ten horns. Then he saw the Ancient of Days sit on his throne in a garment as white as snow, like a flame of burning fire. The judgment was set, and the books were opened; and there came before the Ancient of Days one like a son of man, and dominion was given him over all nations for ever. When the prophet saw these visions he was troubled, and asked one of the Holy Ones who stood by, what was the meaning of these things. He said, "These great beasts are four kingdoms; and after them the kingdom and dominion shall be given to the saints of the Most High for ever." Then two angels stood one on each side of the river of Paradise, shining like fire and girdled with fine gold; and the one cried, "HOW LONG SHALL IT BE?" and the other answered, "BLESSED IS HE WHO HAS PATIENCE UNTIL THE END."

www.ingramcontent.com/pod-product-compliance
Lightning Source LLC
Chambersburg PA
CBHW032054220426
43664CB00008B/997